FLOYD CLYMER'S MOTORCYCLIST'S LIBRARY

The Book of the
VESPA GS AND SS

COMPREHENSIVE MAINTENANCE INSTRUCTIONS
FOR OWNERS OF ALL 1955-67 MODELS

BY

JOHN THORPE

ANNOUNCEMENT

By special arrangement with the original publishers of this book, Sir Isaac Pitman & Son, Ltd., of London, England, we have secured the exclusive publishing rights for this book, as well as all others in THE MOTORCYCLIST'S LIBRARY.

Included in THE MOTORCYCLIST'S LIBRARY are complete instruction manuals covering the care and operation of respective motorcycles and engines; valuable data on speed tuning, and thrilling accounts of motorcycle race events. See listing of available titles elsewhere in this edition.

We consider it a privilege to be able to offer so many fine titles to our customers.

FLOYD CLYMER
Publisher of Books Pertaining to Automobiles and Motorcycles

2125 W. PICO ST. LOS ANGELES 6, CALIF.

INTRODUCTION

Welcome to the world of digital publishing ~ the book you now hold in your hand, while unchanged from the original edition, was printed using the latest state of the art digital technology. The advent of print-on-demand has forever changed the publishing process, never has information been so accessible and it is our hope that this book serves your informational needs for years to come. If this is your first exposure to digital publishing, we hope that you are pleased with the results. Many more titles of interest to the classic automobile and motorcycle enthusiast, collector and restorer are available via our website at www.VelocePress.com. We hope that you find this title as interesting as we do.

NOTE FROM THE PUBLISHER

The information presented is true and complete to the best of our knowledge. All recommendations are made without any guarantees on the part of the author or the publisher, who also disclaim all liability incurred with the use of this information.

TRADEMARKS

We recognize that some words, model names and designations, for example, mentioned herein are the property of the trademark holder. We use them for identification purposes only. This is not an official publication.

INFORMATION ON THE USE OF THIS PUBLICATION

This manual is an invaluable resource for the classic motorcycle enthusiast and a "must have" for owners interested in performing their own maintenance. However, in today's information age we are constantly subject to changes in common practice, new technology, availability of improved materials and increased awareness of chemical toxicity. As such, it is advised that the user consult with an experienced professional prior to undertaking any procedure described herein. While every care has been taken to ensure correctness of information, it is obviously not possible to guarantee complete freedom from errors or omissions or to accept liability arising from such errors or omissions. Therefore, any individual that uses the information contained within, or elects to perform or participate in do-it-yourself repairs or modifications acknowledges that there is a risk factor involved and that the publisher or its associates cannot be held responsible for personal injury or property damage resulting from the use of the information or the outcome of such procedures.

WARNING!

One final word of advice, this publication is intended to be used as a reference guide, and when in doubt the reader should consult with a qualified technician.

PREFACE

EARLY scooters tended to provide a bone-shaking ride, but by the time the G.S. Vespa arrived, in 1955, the bugs were well and truly out of the scooter in general and the Vespa in particular. Here was a scooter which could not only out-perform motor-cycles of equivalent capacity but could also match them on handling, while offering almost complete rider protection. The G.S. became one of my favourite scooters overnight, and has remained so through all the various marks which have ensued in the dozen years since its introduction.

In this book—designed to supplement, but not supplant, the owner's handbook and workshop manuals—I have tried to produce a guide which will help other Vespa enthusiasts to save themselves time, money—and trouble. That means that I have deliberately avoided such jobs as completely stripping the engine/transmission unit, where special tools and special skills are needed. For overhauls of this nature, it is best merely to remove the engine unit from the machine, take off some of the "top hamper," and take the rest of the unit to the nearest fully-equipped agent for attention. That way, you can save a reasonable amount of labour charges without running the danger of damaging expensive components.

This book deals only with the Vespa G.S. and Sports models, from 1955 to 1967. Standard machines are the subject of two separate books—my own *Second Book of the Vespa*, covering those produced from 1959 to 1966; and J. Emmott's *First Book of the Vespa*, dealing with pre-1959 touring scooters. Both books are published by Sir Isaac Pitman & Sons Ltd.

It would be churlish not to acknowledge the help I have received from Douglas (Sales & Service) Ltd., of Kingswood, Bristol—a concern with which I have had close relations both as a journalist and as a user of their products for some 17 years. They have readily granted permission to use material from their official Workshop Manuals, and for the reproduction of their illustrations, and they have checked the proofs and made helpful suggestions for improvements. I am pleased to be able to record my appreciation.

SURRENDEN PARK,
BRIGHTON, SUSSEX.

JOHN THORPE

CONTENTS

CHAPTER		PAGE
1	WORKING ON VESPAS	1
2	HOW THE VESPA WORKS	4
3	TOOLS—AND HOW TO USE THEM	25
4	ROUTINE MAINTENANCE	28
5	WORKING ON VESPA ENGINES	34
6	LOOKING AFTER THE ELECTRICS	47
7	BRAKES, TYRES AND FORKS	53
8	IF IT STOPS...	58
	Appendix: FACTS AND FIGURES	65
	Index	78

CHAPTER ONE

WORKING ON VESPAS

RIGHT from the start of motor-cycling history, manufacturers had tried again and again to produce a machine which would combine at least part of the weather protection of a car with the handiness of the two-wheeler. And again and again they failed. Either the machine gave little protection; or the attempt to fair it in brought grave handling problems; or the open frame proved to be abominably weak and vulnerable.

It took about fifty years for the answer to materialize—and then only as the result of some extremely accurate bombing by the Royal Air Force. They half-wrecked the Piaggio aircraft factory at Pontedera, leaving the staff with a number of headaches. Not least of these was sore feet! The usable parts of the works were few and far between, and getting from one to another was a tiring and time-wasting business. To cut down the footwork, Piaggio designed a little two-wheeled runabout with a 98 c.c. engine, an open footboard, and a small front shield. It was, in fact, the prototype of the Vespa scooter—and with aircraft out of the running as sales were, it didn't take Piaggio long to realize that this diminutive vehicle might provide them with a living once the war was over.

It did. Right from the time of its appearance as a commercial proposition in 1946—with the capacity upped to 125 c.c.—the Vespa sold. It is still selling, and outwardly it is not much changed. Inwardly, though, it's another matter.

The G.S. and Sports Vespas have always been pretty special scooters. Right from the original four-speed 150 c.c. G.S. of 1955 they have been capable of showing most of the opposition a clean pair of wheels, and of giving all the rest a good run for their money. In return, they have asked very little more of their owners than to be cleaned and to have a few minor adjustments carried out regularly.

Normally, your Vespa does not need much in the way of major overhauls. It *does* like a regular "decoke," and appreciates it best at intervals of about 5,000 miles. True, some riders claim to have covered three or more times that distance without disturbing the head, but that is a habit which is officially frowned upon, and which is cheeseparing in the extreme when the simplicity of the work is considered.

After long intervals, you may need to overhaul the clutch, too. This is another fairly simple job providing it is properly tackled. And after a very considerable mileage the engine bearings will need renewal. Here, the work is more complicated but still within the capabilities of the average owner with a reasonable tool kit.

All the rest of the work on a Vespa engine/transmission unit is complicated

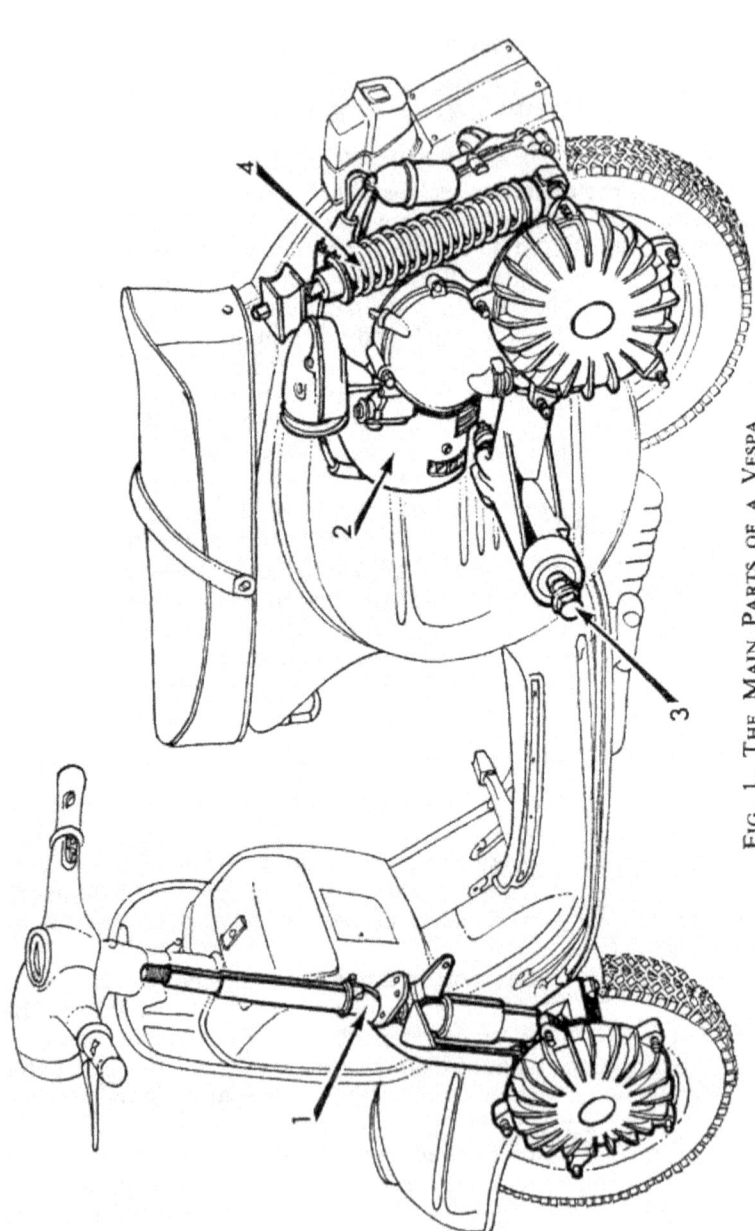

FIG. 1. THE MAIN PARTS OF A VESPA

Conceived as a unit, the Vespa has every component designed especially to match its neighbour. The front fork (1) is of trailing arm design while the engine (2) is horizontal and is mounted on the rear suspension arm (3), which is itself carried on pivots on the body. Its movement is controlled by the spring and damper (4). Both wheel brakes are massively finned for better cooling.

and calls for the use of special tools. Try to "make do" with ordinary hand tools and you are almost certain to damage the mechanism. Therefore, I have deliberately confined myself to describing jobs which the great majority of riders can tackle. The few who wish to go further should acquire the relevant Vespa Workshop Manual and the battery of jigs and presses necessary. They will not, I fear, find it a particularly economic proposition. The main attraction of doing jobs oneself is to save either time or money—and tackling complete stripdowns saves neither.

All work on the scooter must, of course, be carried out very carefully indeed. This is not a machine in which a proprietary engine has been tacked into a frame dreamed up by a snake-charmer and linked to the rear wheel by whatever length of chain happened to fit. Every part of the Vespa is designed to match its neighbour exactly (*see* Fig. 1), and there has been no compromise at all in making the layout right for the job it has to do. So, before you start work on the machine study the relevant chapter thoroughly, until you have the sequence properly memorized. Don't work on a dirty unit, and don't use any but the proper spanners for the job.

Remember, too, that there is an art even in the simplest of tasks. Every spanner is made to a length which, when hand pressure is exerted at the other end, gives just the right leverage to do up a nut or bolt of the appropriate size. Thumping the spanner round with a hammer or trying to increase the leverage by linking two open-enders together will strain or strip threads, and may snap studs or bolts in half—to say nothing of wrecking the spanners. Therefore, beware of over-tightening. It is sufficient if a nut is turned down sufficiently to lock a spring washer fully.

Of the routine jobs you will be carrying out, the most important are those on the braking system. Keep a careful check on your brakes and don't take them for granted. Every day, they lose just a little of their stopping power as the linings gradually lose a fraction of a thou. more "meat." You, being used to the machine, unconsciously adapt yourself to their lessening power. If you are lucky, you don't have to make an emergency stop. If you are unlucky, you do—and that's when you find that they are not half as good as you thought they were. The answer is to test the brakes at least once every week by adopting the "task" system of maintenance outlined in Chapter Four. This is designed to ensure that every important adjustment is checked so frequently that failure from neglect is almost impossible. The cost, in time, is negligible—yet it may save you many pounds.

CHAPTER TWO

HOW THE VESPA WORKS

ALTHOUGH the Vespa, with its long development history, is both efficient and reliable, you must know exactly how and why it works if you are to obtain the best from it (*see* Figs. 2 and 3). This applies not only to the maintenance of the machine, important though that is, but also to its actual use on the road.

So far as engines are concerned, there are two basic types in production for scooters today—the four-stroke engine and the two-stroke. These terms—four-stroke and two-stroke—actually refer to the number of working strokes in one complete cycle of operation of the engine.

In the four-stroke engine, then, the working cycle consists of four strokes; in other words, the piston travels from its uppermost position to its lowest, and vice-versa, four times. In an equivalent two-stroke engine it would make only two such trips. All Vespas have two-stroke engines, but to understand this engine it is best to learn how both types operate.

Before considering just how the engine works, it is necessary to know the names of the components. First there is the *cylinder*, which is, as its name suggests, simply a metal cylinder. It is closed at one end by a *cylinder head*, which, in the case of a four-stroke, is equipped with *ports* through which gas can flow. For each cylinder there is an *inlet port* and an *exhaust port*. These are closed by *valves*, each operated by a form of mechanical see-saw called a *rocker*. In turn, these are operated through an arrangement of *push rods* and *cams*.

The "lower" half of the engine consists of a light alloy case, known as the *crankcase*, on which the cylinder is mounted. Carried on bearings inside the crankcase is the *crankshaft*, usually a pair of heavy flywheels, each with its own half-shaft, joined by a *crankpin*. Though the main shafts are mounted centrally, the crankpin is off-set so that when the crankshaft is revolved the crankpin moves on a circular path. If, then, the crankpin happened to be at the top of the case and the crankshaft was revolved it would not simply rotate, as would the main shafts. Instead it would move at first downward and forward. Once the shaft had been rotated through a right-angle, the pin, while still moving downwards, would begin to move backwards also. After half a turn, it would begin to move upwards and backwards until, in the last quarter-turn, it moved upwards and forwards.

Thus, the end of a *connecting rod* attached to the crankpin would move with the pin in just such a manner. This part of the connecting rod is usually called the *big end*, for the very obvious reason that this particular end of the rod is, invariably, the bigger end.

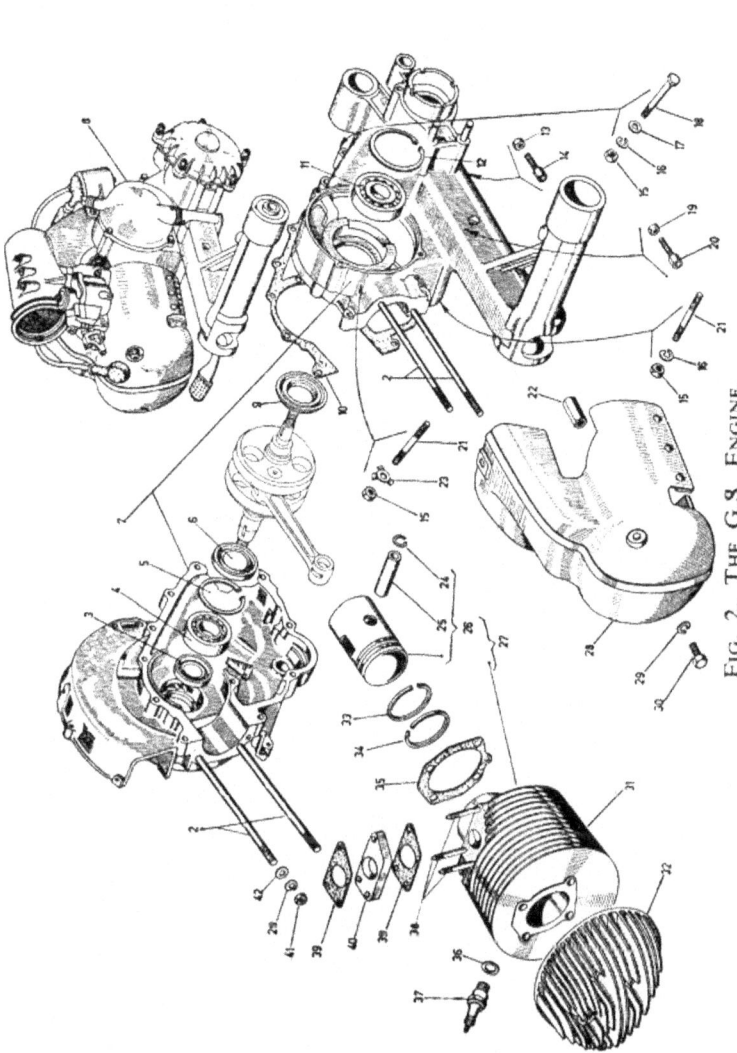

FIG. 2. THE G.S. ENGINE

Comprising the complete engine (8) are the following parts and those shown in Fig. 11 on page 20. They are the four studs (2), external oil seal (3), crankshaft bearing (4), bearing ring (5), oil seal (6), crankcase (7), joint (9), oil seal (10), bearing (11), circlip (12), circlip (13) rear brake adjuster (14), nut (15), spring washer (16), flat washer (17), bolt (18), lock nut (19), clutch cable adjuster (20), five studs (21), distance nut (22), lock washer (23), nut circlip (24), gudgeon pin (25), piston (26), cylinder (27 & 31), cowl (28), spring washer (29), cowl bolt (30), head (32), piston rings (33, 34) base joint (35), plug washer (36), sparking plug (37), carburettor studs (38), joint (39), packing (40), nut (41) and flat washer (42).

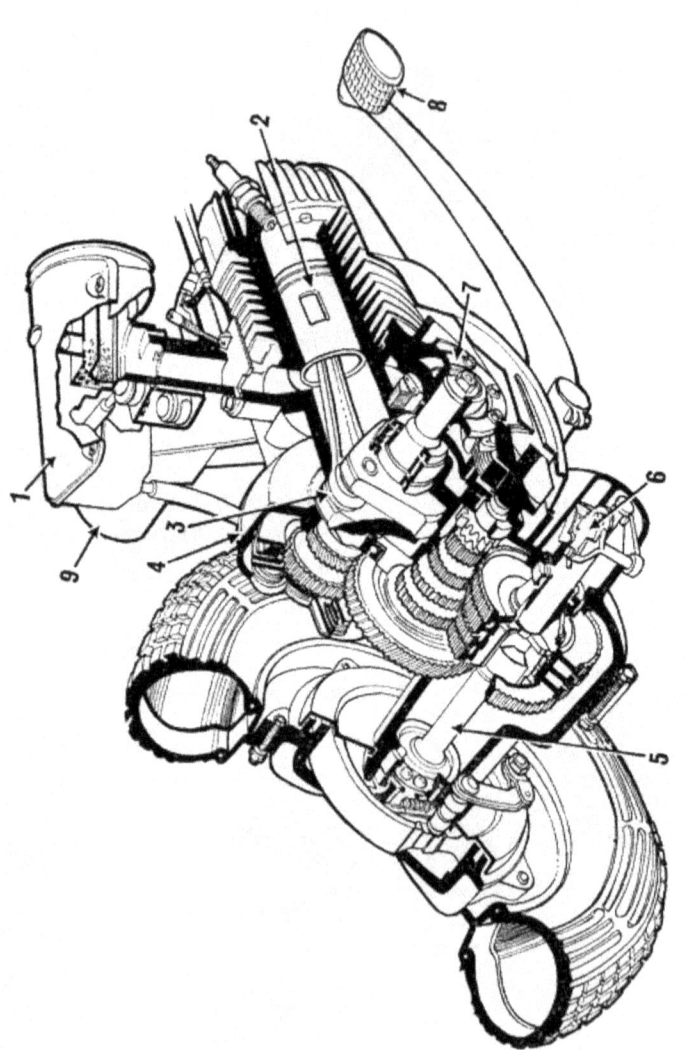

FIG. 3. WHAT'S IN A VESPA ENGINE?

Here is an actual engine cut away to show the internals. The air enters through the air cleaner (1) and after mixing with petrol is induced into the crankcase by movement of the piston (2), which is itself controlled by rotation of the crank assembly (3). Power is transmitted through the clutch (4) to the axle (5) through a choice of gear trains engaged through the selector mechanism (6). Electricity comes from the generator (7).

The other end of the rod—the small end—is also attached to a pin. This is the *gudgeon pin*, and it carries a *piston* made of light alloy. This piston fits closely in the cylinder, in which it is free to slide up and down, but in which it can move in no other way.

If, in this basic engine, the piston is at the top of its travel it is said to be at *top dead centre*—a term usually abbreviated to T.D.C. If it is right at the bottom of its travel it is at *bottom dead centre*, or B.D.C. The distance it must travel between these two points is called the *stroke* and this is normally measured in millimetres.

To understand the four-stroke cycle, imagine that the piston is now at T.D.C. and that the crankshaft is revolving. As it does so, the crankpin moves, at first, downwards and forwards. This means that the big end of the connecting rod must also move downwards and forwards. Since the connecting rod cannot stretch, it exerts a pull on the gudgeon pin, and this in turn pulls the piston downwards. The piston, of course, being a tight fit in the bore, is unable to move forwards or backwards. It can only travel up or down. As the piston moves down the cylinder, the valve which has been closing the inlet port is opened. Inside the cylinder, the movement of the piston has reduced the pressure so that it is lower than that of the air outside, and, therefore, air starts to flow through the inlet port into the cylinder. On its way it is mixed with petrol to form a mixture which can be burned.

This induction of combustible mixture continues for the whole period during which the piston is travelling down the cylinder, and this stroke is consequently called the *induction stroke*.

After half a revolution of the crankshaft, the downward movement of the piston ends, since the crankpin must now begin to press the connecting rod upwards. Obviously, if the inlet port were to be left open, all the mixture which had just been induced would simply be blown out again and the valve is, therefore, so arranged that it closes at this point. The rising piston now compresses the mixture, and this gives the second stroke of the cycle, the *compression stroke*.

By the time the piston reaches T.D.C. on this stroke, the mixture in the cylinder has been squeezed into the tiny "combustion chamber" formed between the top of the piston—the *crown*—and the inside surface of the cylinder head. On a scooter this chamber will have a volume only about one-seventh that of the cylinder itself. The ratio between this and the *swept volume*—the amount of mixture induced into the engine—is called the *compression ratio*, and this is one of the vital factors in deciding the characteristics of an engine. In the case quoted here the compression ratio would be 7 to 1. If the mixture had been compressed into one-tenth of its original volume it would have been 10 to 1.

Once the gas has been so compressed it is ready to be burned. A spark occurs and ignites the mixture, which burns rapidly. In doing so it expands, so that it can no longer be contained within the tiny combustion chamber. It exerts pressure upon every surface around it, but of these only one can move. This is the piston crown, and the effect of igniting the mixture is to create a pressure inside the combustion chamber which thrusts the piston down the cylinder on the third of its four strokes, the *power stroke*. This time, there is no question of the piston being *pulled* down by the crankpin. On the power stroke it is the piston which thrusts the connecting rod down. And the rod, in turn, causes the crankpin to revolve, thereby turning the flywheels and rotating the main shafts. These drive the vehicle through the medium of gears and chains.

One further stroke remains to complete the cycle, the *exhaust stroke*. When the piston reaches B.D.C. the driving force behind it is largely spent.

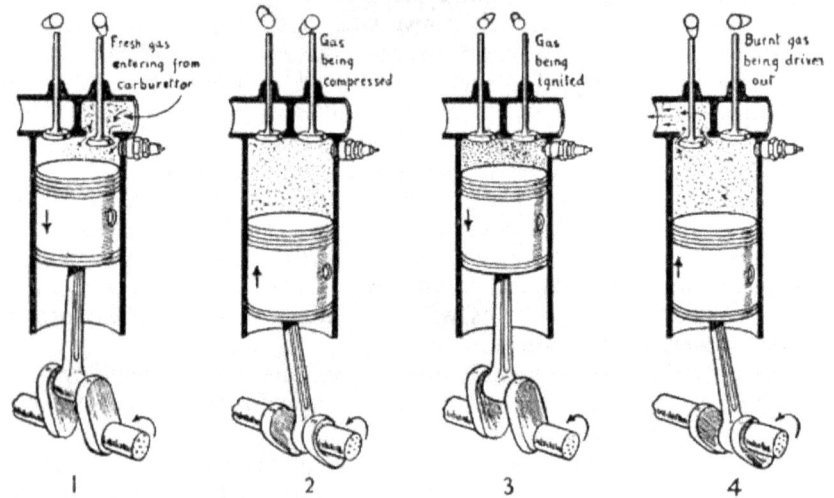

FIG. 4. THE FOUR-STROKE CYCLE

These are the four basic working strokes on which the whole theory of piston engines is based.

Now the burnt gases must be cleared out of the cylinder. Carried by the momentum stored in the flywheels, the piston starts to rise. As it does so, the second valve in the cylinder head—the exhaust valve—is opened. The rising piston pushes the burnt gases up the cylinder and out of the exhaust port. At T.D.C. the exhaust valve again closes the port, the inlet valve opens, the piston begins to descend once more, fresh mixture is induced, and another cycle of operations has begun.

That, then, gives the basic four-stroke cycle: induction, compression, power, exhaust (*see* Fig. 4). Induction and power are downward strokes; compression and exhaust upward strokes. With the two-stroke engine all this is rearranged to occur in only two strokes. The object is to give a smoother-running engine by arranging a power stroke to occur on each downward stroke, whereas the four-stroke only fires on alternate downward strokes. Also the two-stroke is intended to provide an altogether simpler sort of engine (*see* Fig. 5). Like the four-stroke it has a crankcase, crankshaft, cylinder, piston and cylinder head, but it has none of the complicated valve gear necessary to make a four-stroke work.

Paradoxically, although it is so much simpler in construction, it is less simple in its manner of operation, since there are always at least two things happening at once. This stems from the fact that the mixture is not, in the first instance, induced straight into the cylinder but, instead, enters the crankcase, which is made specially gas-tight for this purpose. Since there are no valves—save, on some models, a rotary valve incorporated into the flywheels—all this mixture is distributed through ports which are covered and uncovered by the movement of the piston, and these are consequently located at the base of the cylinder instead of being placed in the cylinder head.

Imagine a two-stroke engine in which the piston is at B.D.C. after a power stroke. At just this moment the last remnants of the burnt gas will still be streaming out of the exhaust port in the base of the cylinder, and two streams of fresh gas entering either through a pair of opposed *transfer ports* or through a single transfer port. These parts connect the crankcase with the cylinder and are usually placed opposite one another so that, as the two gas streams enter the cylinder, they collide and deflect each other upwards, away from the exhaust port. Some Vespas, however, have a piston crown specially shaped to do this job, a type known as a *deflector piston*, and this is used in conjunction with a single transfer port.

The piston now begins to travel up the cylinder. First its upper edge covers the transfer ports, thus sealing the crankcase. Almost immediately afterwards it closes the exhaust port, and the cylinder, too, is sealed. The rising piston now begins to compress the fresh charge trapped in the cylinder, in exactly the same way as in the four-stroke engine.

As the piston nears T.D.C. its lower edge (*skirt*) uncovers the inlet port and a charge is drawn into the crankcase. At T.D.C. a spark occurs in the combustion chamber and the piston is thrust down the cylinder on a power stroke. As it descends it first covers the inlet port with its skirt, and the underside of the piston then begins to compress the mixture in the crankcase.

Towards the end of the stroke the top edge of the piston uncovers the exhaust port, through which the burnt gases are carried by their own momentum. A split second later the top of the piston uncovers the transfer ports, and the underside of the piston begins to pump the fresh charge out of the crankcase, through the transfer ports, and into the cylinder.

When considering the working cycle of the two-stroke, therefore, it is necessary to take into account not only what is happening in the cylinder, *but also what is taking place simultaneously in the crankcase*. Each downward stroke of the piston is a power stroke in the cylinder and a compression stroke in the crankcase. Each upwards stroke of the piston is a compression stroke in the cylinder and an induction stroke in the crankcase. There is no exhaust stroke, this being replaced by a mere phase at the end of the power stroke. The same holds true for the induction stroke so far as the cylinder is concerned, for this is replaced by the transfer period as the piston approaches B.D.C.

Obviously, when an engine is running at a speed which may reach 6,000

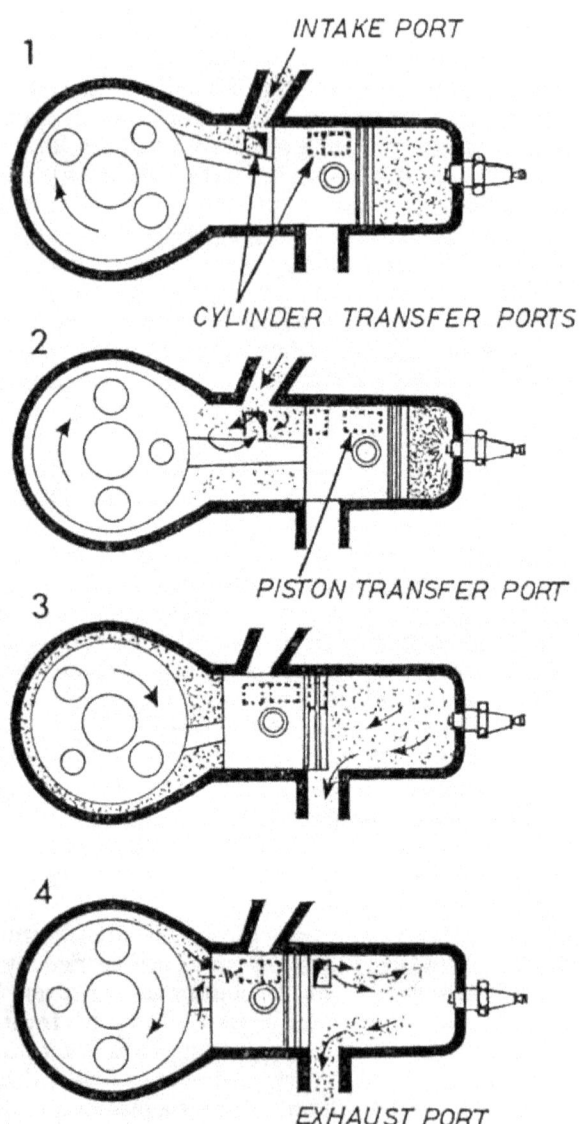

Fig. 5. The Two-Stroke Cycle

In a Vespa engine, which is of two-stroke type, the basic four strokes are telescoped by use of the crankcase for induction. This gives a simpler and smoother-running engine.

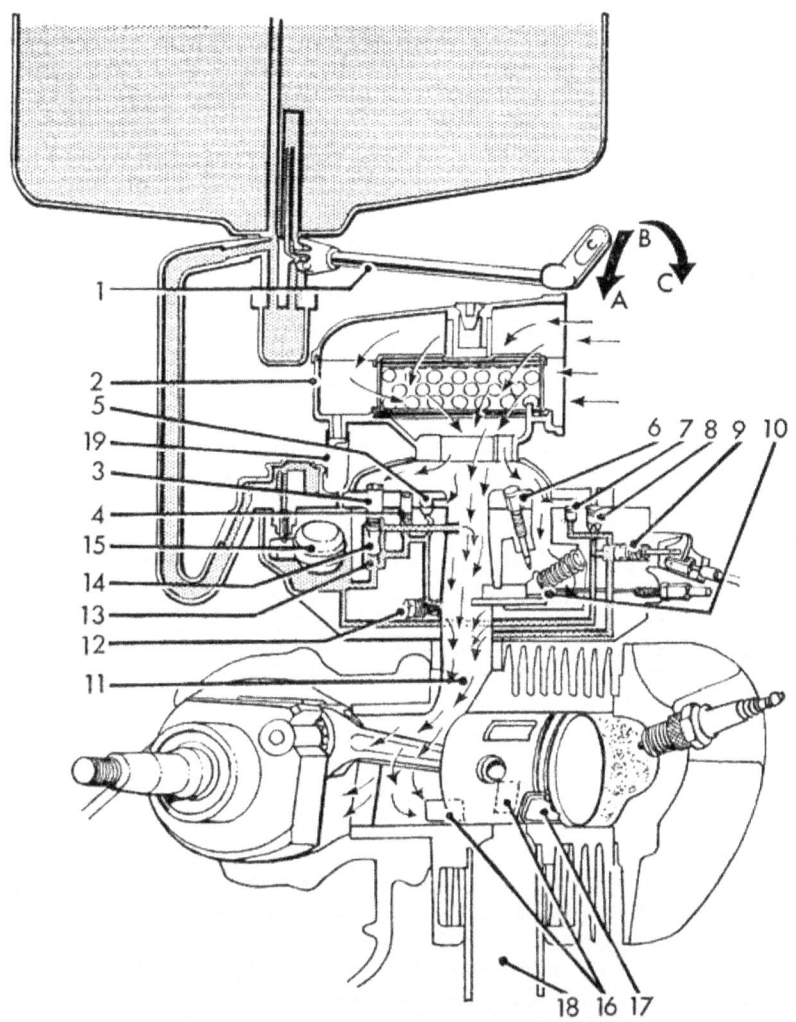

FIG. 6. HOW THE ENGINE BREATHES

Fuel from the tank passes through the three-position fuel tap (1) and air through the filter (2) to the carburettor, where the mixing and metering is done by the air corrector jet (3), slow running jet (4), idling jet air calibrator (5), throttle slide set screw (6), starter jet air calibrator (7), starter jet (8), starter valve (9), throttle slide (10), slow running adjuster screw (12), main jet (13), mixer (14) and the float and chamber (15). From the induction port (11), it passes into the crankcase and into the cylinder through the transfer ports (16), and the piston transfer port (17). After burning, it is expelled through the exhaust port (18). The duct (19) is for excess fuel.

revolutions every minute, there is very little time in which to perform the vital job of clearing the burnt gas out of the cylinder and replacing it with fresh gas. When, as in the two-stroke, one attempts to cram all this "breathing" (*see* Fig. 6) into a few milliseconds at the end of a stroke, some degree of efficiency is bound to be lost, and this, in fact, is precisely what happens.

Since the two-stroke has twice as many power impulses in a given time as the four-stroke, it might be thought that it would develop twice the power from a given size of cylinder. In practice, it usually develops slightly less nominal power than the equivalent four-stroke. One of the reasons is that, at the higher engine speeds, there is this drastically restricted time in which the engine can "breathe." Another reason lies in the construction of the engine itself. The exhaust port *has* to be opened first, and it follows that as the port is piston-controlled it must therefore close *last*. Consequently, it remains open for a short period when the transfers are closed and the piston is ascending. Inevitably, some of the fresh mixture which has just been induced is expelled through the exhaust port and lost.

One aid to greater efficiency is the rotary-valve induction system used on some Vespa models. This enables a longer induction period to be used, yet does not involve complications.

Where the two-stroke really gains is at low engine speeds, since here it has more time to breathe. Consequently, it develops greater usable power than could a four-stroke unit—and this is particularly noticeable on hills. In some cases, as on many of the Vespas, this superiority is so pronounced that the two-stroke engine is able to be operated in conjunction with a three-speed gearbox. But the sports models, of course, have the more complicated four-speed box, allowing for improved acceleration.

Another great simplification which the layout of the two-stroke engine permits is the use of petroil lubrication. All engines need oil. Not only does it reduce friction, but it also helps to keep the internal surfaces relatively cool.

With a four-stroke, it is necessary to use an independent oiling system, fed by a pump which delivers oil from a sump or oil tank, through passageways to bearings, the cylinder walls, and the valve gear. This is, of course, highly efficient, but it calls for the pump itself, its auxiliary drive, and oil container, filters, drain plugs, and passageways.

The two-stroke, however, has its mixture delivered into the crankcase first. If oil is mixed with this fuel, it means that it can be taken into the case and distributed over the bearings and moving parts without any mechanical complication at all. Furthermore, oily mixture is also fed straight into the cylinder from the crankcase, thus giving continual cylinder-wall oiling—by the incoming mixture on the piston's "cylinder compression" stroke, and by the transfer period at the end of the power stroke.

Crude though it may appear at first glance, the petroil system works well in practice, and it has the added advantage that when climbing hills the engine receives an adequate supply of oil, since the amount induced is proportional to throttle opening and not merely to engine speed. On the other hand, when descending a hill with the throttle closed the two-stroke can be partially starved of oil, although enough has usually condensed on the crankcase walls to form an inbuilt reserve which offsets this slight disadvantage.

THE CARBURETTOR

We noted, in passing, that when air is induced into the cylinder it is mixed with fuel to form a combustible mixture. This, of course, is a drastic understatement of the magnitude of the job performed by the simple but precision-engineered instrument known as the carburettor (*see* Figs. 7 and 8).

In principle, this is little more than a glorified scent spray but it has to carry out one of the most crucial of all jobs—metering out a precise and minute ration of fuel and mixing it thoroughly with air in just the right proportion to enable it to burn efficiently.

At first sight, this may not appear to be over-exacting, since the ideal ratio is around 1 part of fuel to 14 parts of air. This, however, is the proportion by *weight*; the carburettor operates by *volume*, and on this basis each 100 c.c. of combustible mixture needs to contain only about 0·2 c.c. of fuel, the remaining 99·8 c.c. being air! Obviously, the carburettor, despite its simplicity, is a precision instrument and has to be treated accordingly.

The basic components of a carburettor are a fuel reservoir, called a *float chamber*; a *venturi* or *choke*, through which air is drawn; *jets*, which meter the fuel; and a *throttle slide*, which controls the amount of mixture which can pass through the carburettor and into the engine.

Consider first the basic method of operation. Fuel is fed to the float chamber. This is very much like a pocket edition of the familiar domestic cistern. The chamber contains a float, which rises as fuel is admitted through a valve. In rising, the float carries with it a tapered needle, and this needle is carefully contoured to fit in a seat in the valve. When the level inside the chamber is correct, the needle is pressed fully home on its seating, thus cutting off the flow of fuel. When the level in the chamber falls the float falls with it, and so does the needle. Leaving its seating, it thus permits more fuel to flow into the chamber, until the correct level is again reached.

Connecting the float chamber with the body of the carburettor is a drilled passageway through which petrol flows into a *jet well*. A tube is placed vertically in this well so that its lower end is immersed, while the upper end opens into the venturi. Screwed to the bottom of this tube is a *jet*, an essential part of the carburettor which looks suspiciously like a small screw or bolt with a hole drilled through the centre. That, in fact, is just what it is, but the hole is so proportioned that it will pass just the right amount of fuel and no more. When the crankcase induction stroke begins, air is drawn through the carburettor venturi, which is so shaped that there is a fall in pressure in the section—called the *mixing chamber*—around the jet

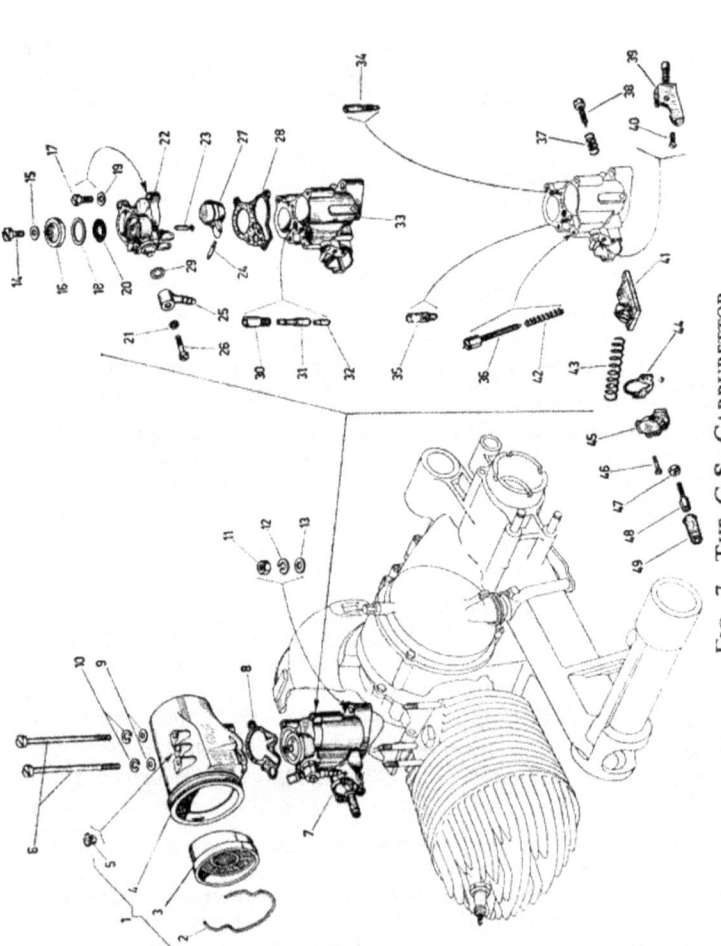

Fig. 7. The G.S. Carburettor

This exploded view shows the construction of the carburettor. The parts are air filter (1) and complete carburetor (7). The components comprise the circlip (2), filter (3), filter body (4), plug (5), two screws (6), joint (8), two flat washers (9), two spring washers (10), three nuts (11), three spring washers (12), three flat washers (13), screw (14), seal (15), screw (16), two screws (17), gasket (18), two washers (19), petrol filter (20), washer (21), chamber cover (22), float needle (23), pin (24), banjo union (25), screw (26), float (27), joint (28), washer (29), screw (30), emulsion tube (31), main jet (32), carburettor body (33), pilot jet (34), starter jet (35), screw (36), spring (37), screw (38), starter (39), screw (40), valve (41), spring (42), valve spring (43), joint (44), valve cover (45), screw (46), adjuster lock nut (47), cable adjuster (48) and adjuster cap (49).

tube. As a result, fuel is drawn up the tube into the chamber, where it mixes with the air, and passes through the inlet port into the crankcase.

Obviously, a carburettor which consisted of these parts alone would work, but the engine would run at only one speed. Some means of varying the supply of mixture has to be arranged, and this means has to be one which keeps the essential fuel-air proportion at all openings.

On earlier Vespas, the solution adopted was to use a *needle jet* to control

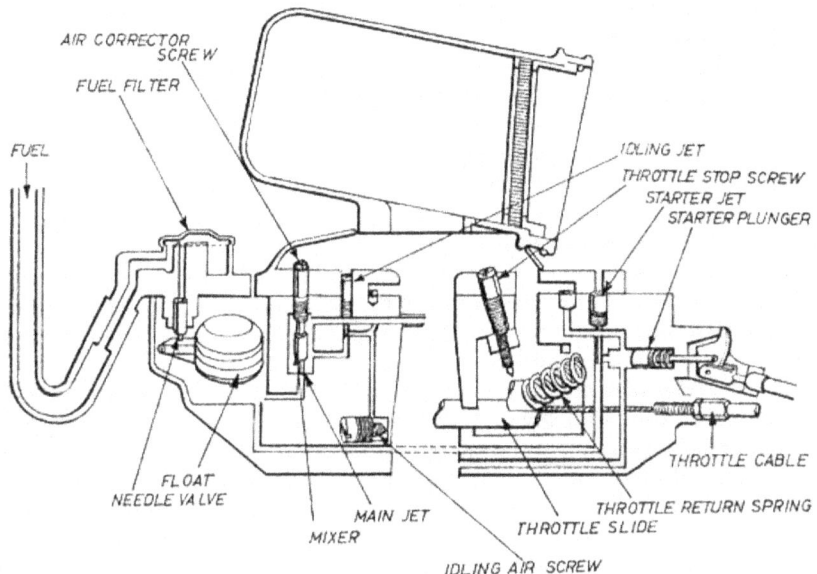

FIG. 8. A CARBURETTOR IN CROSS SECTION

This diagrammatic cross-section shows one of the later-type Dell' Orto carburettors in which no needle jet is used. When renovating or cleaning one of these, remove only one jet at a time to avoid confusion on reassembly.

the fuel flow into the mixing chamber, and to couple this to a *throttle slide* to vary the amount of air admitted. This is how such a system works.

The jet tube is carefully tapered internally to match a long, tapered needle, arranged to move inside it. At the top, this needle is clipped to the air slide, which is itself capable of moving up and down in the carburettor. A cable, connected to the throttle control, pulls it upwards, and a light spring helps to return it when the control is slackened.

At the front of the slide a half-moon shaped area is cut away, and it is this *cut-away* which governs the characteristics of the slide and decides how much air can pass through it at intermediate throttle openings.

When the throttle is closed, only a very small amount of air can pass—so small, in fact, that it is impossible for the main jet to meter out the tiny amount of fuel required. For running under these conditions a very fine jet, called, the *pilot jet*, delivers a minute ration of fuel to the mixing chamber, and in the main jet itself the throttle needle is hard against its seating, and no fuel at all passes through.

As the throttle is opened, the slide is raised, and so is the needle. More air passes through the venturi, and the movement of the tapered needle has opened up a passage for fuel through the main jet. Further movement of the throttle increases both the amount of air permitted to pass and the amount of fuel which the jet supplies, until at full throttle both passages supply the maximum amounts of which they are capable. Later carburettors retain the slide, but use internal metering jets in place of the needle and jet tube.

Since the proper action of the carburettor depends upon the operation of very fine metering devices, great attention must be paid to ensuring that the internals are kept free of dirt. Even a speck of dirt is quite enough to block the jet and thus prevent fuel passing through it. The petrol is, therefore, normally filtered at several points by passing through fine wire mesh. One such filter is usually fitted round the inlet of the on/off tap, in the fuel tank, and a second filter protects the needle valve.

When an engine is cold it needs a somewhat richer mixture than usual to enable it to start, and to supply this it is usual to employ a *strangler*, sometimes called, rather misleadingly, a *choke*. This should not, of course, be confused with the venturi.

The purpose of a strangler is to cut down the air supply independently of the fuel supply, thus giving the same amount of fuel but mixing it with a smaller supply of air: and a rich-mixture device of this type is invariably some form of plate, which is used to block the carburettor inlet. It can be a supplementary slide, a plate which swings over the mouth of the carburettor, or even a form of shutter on the carburettor air filter. A variation is to use a starter unit, which richens the mixture without cutting the air supply.

All Vespa carburettors, besides being equipped with fuel filters, also have a filter for the air. This is not so much to protect the carburettor as to protect the engine, since the air usually contains dust; and dust, harmless though it may look, contains a surprising number of very hard particles which are quite capable of scratching the working parts of the engine very badly indeed.

An air filter itself forms an obstacle to the air flow and cuts the amount of air entering the carburettor. In the design stage this obstruction is taken into consideration, and the fuel is metered accordingly. If, therefore, an instrument which is intended to have an air filter is used without one the effect is to weaken the resulting mixture, since more air is entering while the fuel supply remains unaltered. Damage to the internal parts of the engine apart, this is one reason why the engine should not be run with the air filter removed.

THE IGNITION SYSTEM

Even really experienced riders often have only the slightest knowledge of the working of the electrical system upon which the whole operation of the engine depends. As a result, the electrics are frequently neglected, failure results—and the immediate conclusion is that electricity is thoroughly unreliable anyway! There is no need, however, to be a qualified electrical engineer to understand *how* the system works (*see* Fig. 9).

All electrical practice is founded upon *circuits*, and upon the fact that an electric current will invariably take the shortest path to earth. In this connexion, though, it should be emphasized that "earth" does not necessarily mean the ground. So far as a scooter's electrical system is

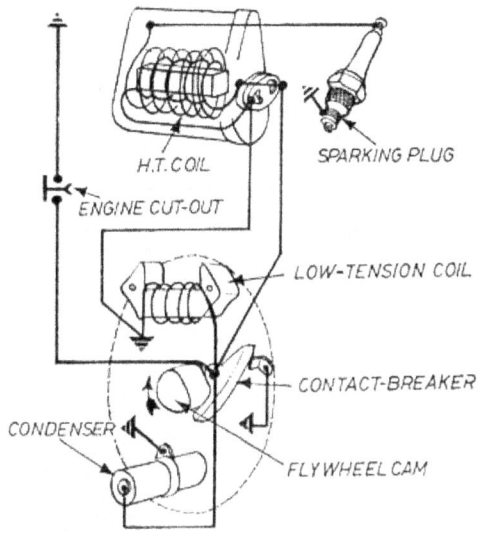

FIG. 9. THE IGNITION CIRCUIT

This diagram shows the layout of the Vespa's ignition components and how they are connected.

concerned, "earth" is the mass of the scooter itself, a little world all of its own.

A circuit is just what its name implies. In this, electricity is rather like a model railway. If all the points are correctly set, the train will go round and round. If they are not so set, it will simply end up standing still.

As with the train, so with electricity. Provided there is a circuit, the current will flow. If the circuit is broken, it will not. And just occasionally there may be some points badly set which direct it straight to earth—a *short-circuit*—just as if the train had been directed on to a branch line leading straight to a siding.

Electricity is measured in *volts* and *amperes*. The *volt* is a measure of its force: the *ampere* basically a measure of the number of electrons per second passing a given point within the electrical circuit. In other words, while voltage indicates the electrical pressure in the circuit, amperes indicate the *quantity* of electricity which is flowing. The resistance to the flow presented by the wires and so forth which make up the circuit is measured in *ohms*, one ohm being a resistance which calls for one volt to be applied so that one ampere may flow.

Electricity is further regarded as comprising two basic types of current—*positive* and *negative*—but for all practical purposes it is only necessary to know that these do, in fact, exist.

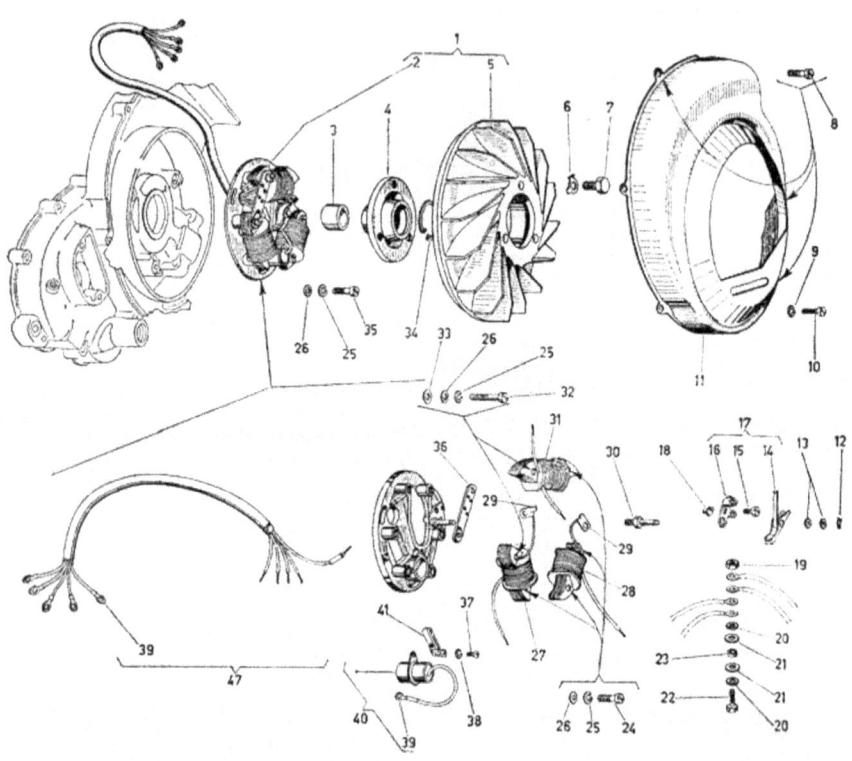

FIG. 10. THE FLYWHEEL MAGNETO

The components of the Vespa generator (1) are the stator assembly (2) the cam (3), the flywheel centre rotor (4), the flywheel fan (5), three lockwashers and screws (6 & 7), four screws (8), spring washer (9), two fan-securing screws (10) the fan cover (11), a clip (12), two to five shims (13), the contact arm (14), bracket screw (15), contact plate (16), contact-breaker complete (17), eccentric screw (18) nut (19), washers (20 & 21), screw (22), ring (23), coil-fixing screws (24), nine spring washers (25), nine flat washers (26), No. 1 coil (27) No. 2 coil (28), two tags (29), pivot (30), H.T. coil (31), two screws and washers (32, 33), circlip (34), three stator plate screws (35), terminal (36), condensor fixing screw (37), spring washer (38), six tags (39), condensor (40), lubricating pad (41) and loom (47).

Finally it is necessary to accept one further basic fact: that when a *coil* is placed in a magnetic field electricity is produced.

Two types of machine for producing electricity are used on engines—the a.c. generator and the d.c. generator. The first produces an *alternating current*, one which has a constantly reversing flow. The second produces *direct current*, which flows in one direction only. On Vespas a d.c. flywheel magneto-generator (*see* Fig. 10) is employed.

In this design permanent magnets are mounted inside the rim of the external flywheel, and a stator plate, bolted to the engine, holds an ignition coil and lighting coils, each being closely-wound coils of fine wire. They are different, however, in that the ignition coil is really two coils in one—a low-tension primary winding surrounding a high-tension secondary winding, but fully insulated from it. Sometimes this high-tension coil is mounted externally and current is fed from low-tension coils on the stator plate.

There is one other essential part: the *contact-breaker*. This is simply a mechanical switch, consisting of a pair of points which are opened and closed by a cam carried on the engine mainshaft. Electrically, the contact-breaker is connected into the low-tension side of the ignition circuit.

From the high-tension winding of the ignition coil, a heavily insulated *high-tension lead* is connected to a *sparking plug* set in the cylinder head. This plug consists of a *body*, which screws into the head, and an insulated central *electrode* to which the high-tension lead is connected. Welded to the body is a *side electrode*—some plugs may have several—which is set so that a gap of around 20 thousandths of an inch exists between its tip and that of the central electrode.

When the flywheel is revolved, the magnets set up a magnetic field, and low-tension electricity is generated in the primary windings of the ignition coil. At a predetermined point, however, the cam presses one of the points of the contact-breaker away from the other, and thus breaks the circuit.

Here something happens which has to be taken on trust. This sudden rupturing of the low-tension circuit in the primary windings of the ignition coil creates a high-tension current in the coil's secondary windings. This current is of a very high voltage—about 16,000 volts. Seeking the shortest path to earth, this current streaks down the high-tension lead. Normally it would stop dead at the gap in the sparking plug, but the pressure behind it is too great to permit it to do so. Instead, it jumps across the gap in the form of a hot, blue spark, and it is this spark which ignites the mixture in the cylinder. In a normal scooter two-stroke engine this operation can occur over 5,000 times every minute.

To prevent the low-tension current from doing at the contact-breaker points just what the high-tension current subsequently does at the sparking-plug gap—jumping across in the form of a spark—a small electrical "shock absorber" called a condenser is added to the circuit.

The lighting systems and horn can be supplied with electricity from a battery, which is charged by current delivered from the L.T. coils, or this current can be taken direct to the components concerned, which will then operate only when the engine is running.

THE TRANSMISSION

Internal-combustion motors are high-speed engines in which power output is, within limits, proportional to the speed of rotation of the engine. At low speeds, therefore, less power is developed than at high speeds. Where outside factors—such as a hill—increase the load on an engine its speed, and consequently its power, falls off. This, in turn, reduces its speed still more, causing a further drop in power. At length, the load becomes so great that it overcomes the remaining power of the engine and the motor "stalls."

Basically, there is a comparatively narrow range of engine speed at which the greatest power is developed, and the engine should, ideally, run at this speed whenever possible. The designer does in fact try to arrange for this to coincide with the top-gear cruising speed. To deal with varying loads, however, some means of keeping engine speed high when road speed falls is necessary, and this need is met by the gearbox.

This consists basically of *input* and *output* shafts, on which are carried a series of meshing gears. Each pair of gears gives a different reduction between the speeds of the two shafts. Only one pair of gears can be used to transmit the power at any one time.

Initially, the *primary drive* which transmits the crankshaft movement to the gearbox, provides the first reduction in speed, cutting the rotational speed by approximately one half. This is reduced still further in the gearbox itself, depending upon which pair of gears is locked into position on the shafts. In top gear, therefore, the engine crankshaft may revolve four times for each revolution of the rear wheel, but in bottom gear it will turn over 12 times. In one revolution of the rear wheel, then, top gear allows the power of four power strokes to be applied. But in bottom gear—in the same distance covered—the power of 12 strokes is passed through to the driving wheel. Thus an increase in load can be counterbalanced by changing into a lower gear, bringing more power to bear in a given distance at the cost of a drop in road speed.

The method employed to lock the various gears to the shafts is supremely simple. On the input shaft all gears revolve with the shaft; on the output shaft the gears run free, but are constantly meshed with the input gears. Each free-running gear in turn can be locked to the shaft when a sliding member is moved sideways by a *selector*, whose movement is dictated by a twist grip and cable control.

A vital part of the transmission is the *clutch*, which enables the drive to be freed at will (*see* Fig. 11). A clutch consists of one member driven by the engine, a second member which is connected to the transmission, and *friction plates* which link the two, together with springs and a withdrawal mechanism. There is thus no direct connexion between the engine and the transmission. All the drive is taken through the clutch plates. The clutch has two main parts: the *clutch centre* and the *clutch body*.

The clutch centre has a series of splines on its boss, and the clutch body a series of splines round its inner periphery. Inside, a *pressure plate* and a

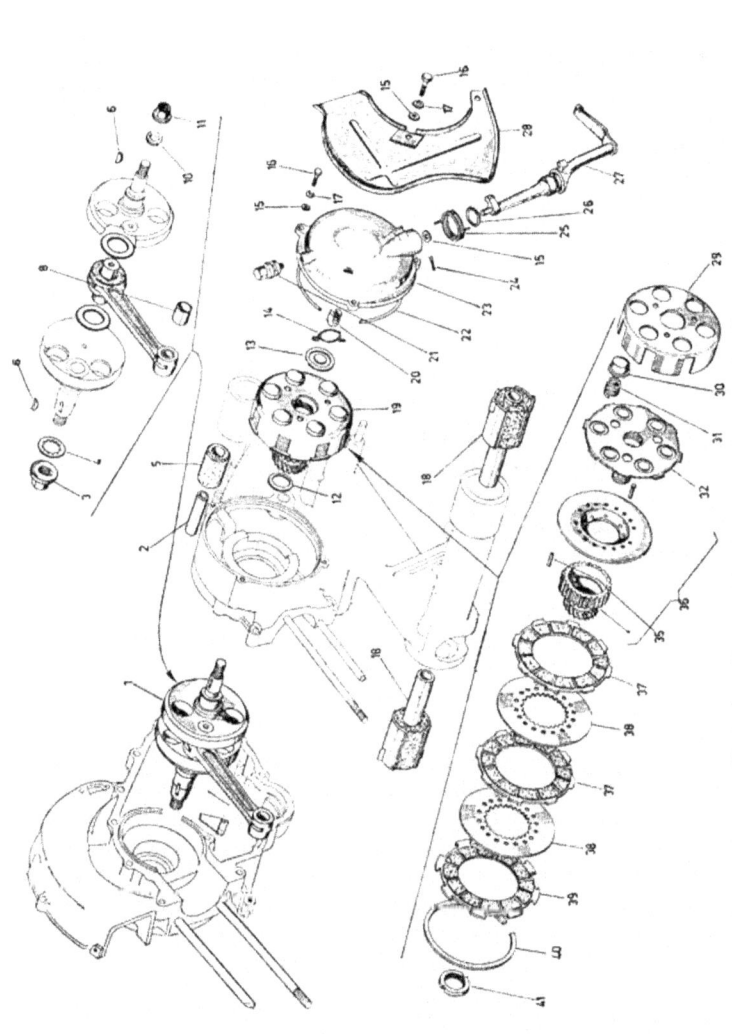

FIG. 11. THE G.S. CRANKSHAFT AND CLUTCH

Shown here are the crankshaft complete (1), tube (2), flywheel securing nut (3), washer (4), bush (5), clutch and flywheel keys (6), small end bush (8), spring washer (10), clutch nut (11), thrust washer (12), clutch centralizing plate (13), circlip (14), flat washer (15), clutch cover screws (16), spring washer (17), bush (18), complete clutch (19), clutch plunger (20), breather (21), clutch cover sealing ring (22), split pin (24), return spring (25), seal (26), clutch operating lever (27), shield (28), clutch housing (29), clutch cup (30), clutch body (31), clutch rollers (32), clutch spring (35), clutch gear and plate assembly (36) corked inner plate (37), convex plate (38), outer corked plate (39), circlip (40), ring (41). See also Fig. 2 on page 5.

series of *clutch plates* are fitted. Half these carry friction linings. Alternate plates are splined round the outer edge to match the splining of the clutch body. Strong springs, held by a spring plate, press all these plates hard together. When the clutch is driven by the crankshaft it turns and, owing to the pressure exerted by the springs, the friction between the plates is such that they also turn as one unit and in so doing transmit the drive.

When the withdrawal mechanism is operated the pressure of the springs is relieved. The part of the clutch driven from the engine—and the plates fixed to it—still revolve, but the friction between these and the remaining plates is now too low to transmit movement. The lined plates therefore remain stationary, and so does that part of the clutch fixed to the primary drive. Thus, no drive is transmitted.

By gradually releasing the withdrawal mechanism, the revolving plates can be brought into gradual contact with the stationary plates. At first, these "slip," but as contact is increased they speed up, until with the full spring pressure restored the whole clutch is once again rotating as a complete unit. This is what happens each time a scooter moves off from a standstill.

THE CYCLE PARTS

When a scooter is driven along a road it remains upright for exactly the same reason that a gyroscope refuses to topple over; the two revolving wheels do, in effect, act as a pair of gyroscopes, and resist all atempts to force them out of their course.

There are, however, other factors which enter into it. One is the design of the steering gear. This is so arranged that, although the fact is not immediately apparent, the front wheel is trailing rather like the castor of an armchair. The characteristics of the steering depend to some extent upon the amount of *trail* specified by the designer, and to some extent upon other factors. One of these is the *rake*—the angle at which the steering head is set—and others are the weight distribution of the machine as a whole and the position of its centre of gravity.

In addition, the manner in which the suspension systems act plays a great part in determining whether the scooter handles well or not. The Vespa design utilizes a trailing link front fork, in which a short arm carrying the wheel moves upwards and backwards against the resistance of a spring. This movement has to be damped. If there were no damper, the spring would thrust the wheel up and down with a rapid action, and so cause the front end of the machine to pitch up and down. That's just what did happen on very early models. . . .

To prevent this, a *hydraulic damper* is used. It consists of an oil chamber, found in the lower sliding member of a telescopic unit, and a disc valve, so designed that when the sliding member rises it permits the oil to pass through with little or no resistance. On the return stroke the valve is partially closed, and this slows down the rate at which the oil can return to the chamber, causing considerable friction through oil drag. In consequence, the return stroke of the trailing link is also slowed down,

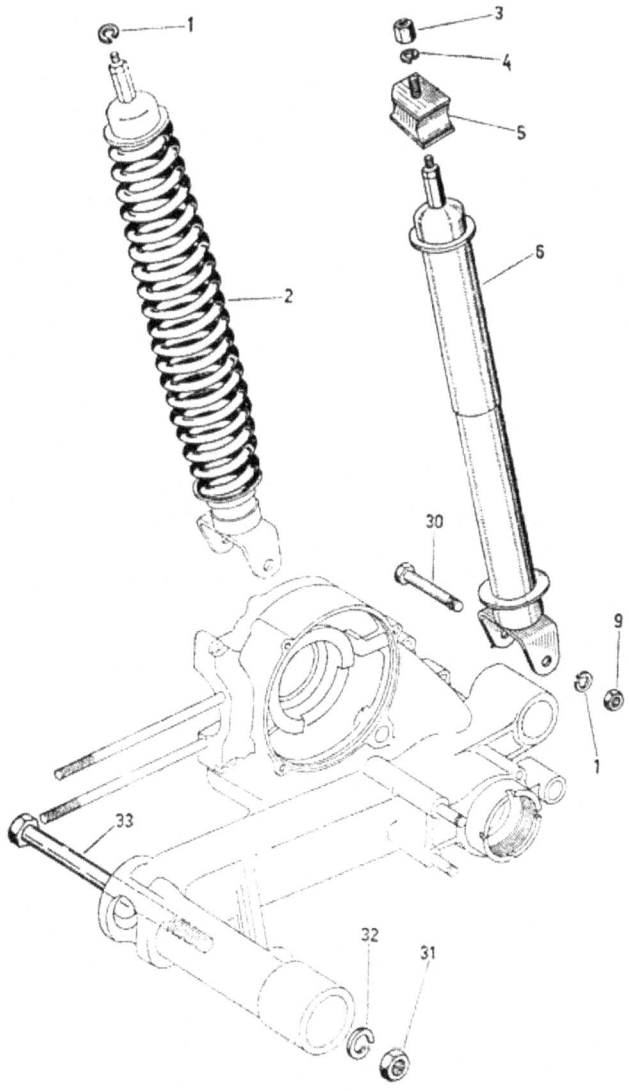

FIG. 12. REAR SUSPENSION

Shown in this exploded view of a typical suspension are the spring washers (1, 4, 32), suspension spring (2), nuts (3, 9, 31), bolts (30, 33), rubber mounting (5), rear damper (6). This assembly is part of the engine, and these are the parts which must be unbolted when the unit is being removed.

thereby preventing spring oscillation. A similar layout is adopted at the rear, where the suspension is controlled by a large coil spring and an independent hydraulic damper (*see* Fig. 12).

Just as important as making the scooter move is the ability to make it stop. This is the job of the brakes, which are of the internal-expanding type. Each wheel carries a *drum*, the inside surfaces of which are accurately ground so that the drum is completely round and true.

Closing the drum is a *back-plate*, and affixed to this plate is a *pivot pin*. Diametrically opposed to the pin is a cam, which is connected to the brake lever. Two *brake shoes*—semi-circular in shape, with a friction lining riveted to the outer curve on each—are fitted with one end butting on the pivot pin and the other on one face of the cam. They are held together by a spring and the whole back-plate assembly is fixed rigidly to the machine.

When the brake lever or pedal is operated, the cam turns and presses the free ends of the shoes outwards. This brings the friction linings into contact with the inside surface of the drum, decelerating the machine.

A brake is basically a form of heat exchanger. The friction created by the linings rubbing on the surface of the drum absorbs energy which would otherwise be devoted to driving the scooter, and this energy is converted into heat, which is dissipated from the surface of the drum.

Both brakes on Vespas are controlled by cables. In addition, cables are used for the throttle, clutch and gear controls. For efficient operation, a cable depends upon the correct relationship between its inner and outer wires being maintained. Since the inner wires have a tendency to stretch, the outer casings are provided with screwed adjusters which enable the effective length of the outer casing to be varied in relation to the inner wire. All cables work either against the resistance of a spring, by which the return action is supplied, or against the pull of a second cable operating in an opposite direction, since cables normally perform well only when used in tension.

CHAPTER THREE

TOOLS—AND HOW TO USE THEM

It is virtually impossible to make a bigger mistake, when setting out to maintain or overhaul a scooter, than to attempt to do the job with inadequate tools. To carry out even routine maintenance jobs properly calls for the use of a good-quality tool kit, while major overhauls quite often require the use of special tools. This is certainly the case with the Vespa, since stripping demands the use of tools designed by the manufacturer to do one specific job—and one job only.

Each Vespa is equipped with a tool kit upon delivery, but this is designed to cope only with roadside emergencies and to carry out the major routine jobs. It is not intended for the sterner work of stripping the engine.

The use of special service tools for such jobs as splitting the crankcases is not dictated by cantankerousness on the part of the manufacturer; nor does it indicate a desire to make a little on the side by selling such tools at an extra profit. It merely reflects the fact that these scooters are precision-engineered. To obtain the performance and reliability of the Vespa the specified tolerances are very close. Use of special tools helps to preserve them by guarding against damage during stripping and reassembly.

Even where the jobs to be tackled do not call for the use of special tools they will still require the use of good tools. Cheap spanners and so forth are a bad investment. They do not wear well, and they also have an infuriating habit of ruining nuts and bolts. Thus, the first essential is to buy a really good set of chrome-vanadium open-ended spanners in metric sizes. A set of half a dozen spanners will give a range of sizes sufficient for most of the work, and will cost only a couple of pounds.

Next, it is vital to have a set of strong metric box spanners—or, better still, socket spanners. Ring spanners are more of a luxury. They are less handy in confined spaces than are open-enders or sockets, although they do give a very good grip. In addition, you will need a pair of really good screwdrivers, with insulated handles. One screwdriver with a 5/16-in. blade and an electrical screwdriver with a long 1/8-in. blade are the minimum requirements. And don't forget your pliers. They are indispensable for electrical work and for use on the control cables.

USING THE TOOLS

There is far more to using even the simplest of hand tools than merely placing them in position and tugging hard. Each particular type of spanner has its own characteristics, and each is better suited to one particular type of job. The factory places great stress on using the right tools for every operation.

Open-ended spanners are the great all-rounders of the kit. They can be used in confined spaces and they have the advantage that the jaws are angled, so that reversing the spanner will give fresh purchase on the nut. This is most useful when the nut in question is somewhat inaccessible, since it can be freed in stages simply by constantly reversing the spanner.

It is, of course, essential that only the right size of spanner should be used. The open-ender applies its pressure on the flats of the nut or bolt, and is consequently made with jaws of just the right width to grip them. If too large a spanner is used the jaws will press against the angles of the bolt instead of the flats. One of two things then happens: either the spanner gouges away the metal of the head, leaving a rounded surface which no spanner on earth could ever again grip, or else the bolt head slightly springs the jaws of the spanner itself, which is promptly ruined. Or, of course, you can get the worst of both worlds and ruin both bolt and spanner together!

Damage to the jaws can also be caused by applying excessive force when trying to free a bolt which refuses to budge. There is a temptation, under these circumstances, to slip a piece of piping over the free end of the spanner to increase the leverage. This is permissible in an emergency, provided due care is used, but if you are none too experienced as a mechanic it is inadvisable to try it. You are more likely to spring the spanner's jaws or snap the bolt. Use a socket spanner instead and you will be surprised at the result.

Socket, box, or ring spanners are at a great advantage when it comes to shifting recalcitrant nuts. Rings and sockets both grip on the angles, not the flats, of the bolt and consequently apply pressure at half a dozen points where the open-ended spanner can do so only on two surfaces. A box spanner can apply its force on both angles and flats provided it fits well (cheap box spanners rarely do) but frequently the weak point here is the tommy bar used to turn the box, which simply bends under the strain. Another drawback with box spanners is that, owing to the offset between the part of the spanner which holds the nut and the holes through which the tommy bar passes, the spanner may tend to ride off the hexagon when pressure is applied.

When using a spanner to tighten nuts or bolts it is important to remember that too much force should not be used. Spanners are made long enough to ensure that mere hand pressure applied through the full leverage of the spanner is sufficient to lock the size of nut or bolt for which the spanner is intended. If excessive force is used, the actual material of the bolt can be weakened sufficiently to cause a fracture. This point, too, should be borne in mind particularly when tightening bolts which are threaded into light alloy. Here, the steel bolt is much harder than the material forming the internal threads, and over-enthusiasm with the spanner can easily strip the threads in the hole. The only real solution, then, is to drill out the hole and re-tap it to take a larger-sized bolt.

Pliers, of course, should never be used as a makeshift spanner, since the jaws can never be parallel and the serrated pipe grip is almost perilously liable to slip. A rounded hexagon is the inevitable result if it does.

Adjustable spanners should never be allowed near the machine. They are a butcher's tool, not a mechanic's. True, an "adjustable" can be useful in an emergency—but for workshop maintenance it is best forgotten since, again, the jaws can never be aligned accurately enough to obviate the danger of slipping.

Screwdrivers should have their blades properly ground so that, in side view, the blade is at first concave, and then runs parallel all the way to the tip. This enables it to be seated properly in the slot and to apply its pressure evenly. A screwdriver whose blade is wedge-shaped when viewed from the side cannot seat properly and exerts all its force on the edges of the slot. Understandably, these crumble under the strain, and the screw is useless thereafter.

After use, all tools should be wiped clean, kept in a dry place, and protected from dust by being wrapped in rag. If they are used fairly infrequently they should also be very lightly oiled. The film of lubrication should, of course, be wiped off before they are used again.

CHAPTER FOUR

ROUTINE MAINTENANCE

THERE is, obviously, a difference between routine maintenance—the day-to-day adjustment and minor repairs which all vehicles need—and major overhauls, but both have their place in keeping a scooter in good working order. A scooter repays constant and sympathetic attention to its everyday condition, but certainly does not take kindly to constant stripping of the engine. Oddly, many owners fall into the error of neglecting to give their machines minor attention, while over-conscientiously pulling them apart two or three times each year.

This is the exact opposite of the correct approach. Well driven, and properly maintained, a Vespa will cover about 5,000 miles before a top overhaul (a couple of hours' job) is recommended. Some riders have covered well over 10,000 miles without decarbonizing, but the manufacturers frown on such mileages before the engine is attended to. The machine *can* do it; but should not be asked to.

If the routine maintenance is neglected, however, the time which can elapse between overhauls is drastically shortened and the amount of work needing to be done (and the amount of money which needs to be spent) will be much increased.

The reason for this is simple enough. Maladjustments have a cumulative effect. Little enough harm, for example, will result if a sparking plug is loose and the scooter covers 20 miles or so before the fault is discovered. But if, in the absence of a routine check, the loose plug is left for a thousand miles, the results can be serious. All sorts of troubles could spring from this one minor example of neglect. Hot gases could burn away the lower threads in the plug hole, and the wobbling plug could elongate the hole itself. Since the compression would be reduced the engine could never develop its full power, so the performance would fall and the fuel consumption would rise. Extra air drawn in through the plug hole would give a weak mixture, so causing overheating and possible distortion of the barrel and piston. Seizure might result. At the very least, a new head might be required. At worst, you might find yourself paying for a new head, barrel and piston. A pretty stiff price, that, for the minute saved by omitting to make a single, simple check.

Or consider the case of the brakes, which gradually deteriorate in their performance. Unless their power and adjustment is constantly checked you may easily find that when an emergency stop has to be made in a distance of forty feet the scooter will not stop in less than forty-five. The result can be very expensive indeed. It is a dangerously unnecessary way of learning a lesson.

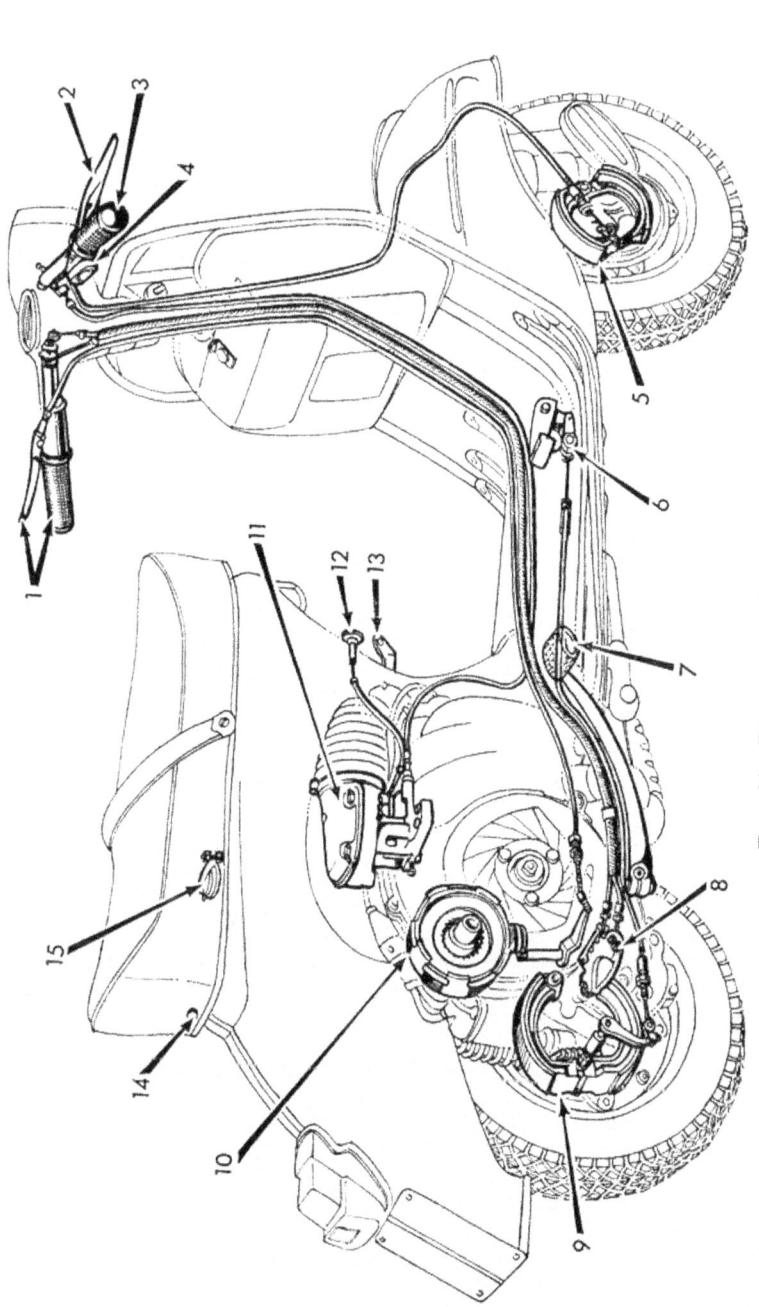

Fig. 13. Points for Attention

When maintaining your Vespa, make sure that all of these are checked for security, freedom of action, and lubrication where appropriate: 1. Clutch control and clutch-side handlebar grip; 2. Front brake control; 3. Twist grip throttle; 4. Switch; 5. Front brake; 6. Rear brake pedal; 7. Starter pedal rubber; 8. Gear selection mechanism; 9. Rear brake mechanism; 10. Clutch; 11. Carburettor; 12. Starter control; 13. Fuel tap; 14. Dualseat press-button; 15. Tank filler cap vent.

TASK SYSTEMS

Constant and methodical inspection is the best way of preventing troubles, but the usual recommendations, based on elapsed mileage, are difficult to carry out if a full log of the work already done is not kept. This was a problem which faced the armed forces some years ago, and to combat it the military authorities evolved task systems which called for a daily or weekly check on each aspect of the mechanical side of a vehicle.

In a modified form such systems are ideally suited for a privately-owned and maintained scooter. They can be of two types, daily or weekly. Which is employed depends entirely on the use to which the scooter is put. If it is a "ride to work" machine, checks could be made each day. If it is employed solely for week-end excursions, a weekly basis can be substituted.

Taking the daily system first, here is a maintenance check routine for Vespas. It is designed to cover all the major parts which need to be checked—but to carry out these recommendations should never involve the expenditure of more than ten minutes in a single day. In most cases, only a couple of minutes will be needed.

DAILY SYSTEMS

Sunday: check the adjustment of front and rear brakes; check freedom of action of brake controls; check security of nuts and bolts in braking system; check lubrication of brake cables.

Monday: check gearbox oil level; check all controls for free movement and adequate lubrication.

Tuesday: check sparking plug for gap and condition; check battery.

Wednesday: examine tyre treads and remove any trapped stones; check tyre pressures; check wheels for security; rock wheels and front fork to check play in bearings.

Thursday: check clutch cable for adjustment; check that clutch plates are freeing.

Friday: check all nuts and bolts for security; check petrol flow.

Saturday: check all exposed electrical wiring for signs of abrasion or fracture; check all electrical terminals for tightness; check operation of horn, lamps and dip-switch; check contact-breaker setting.

ALTERNATIVE WEEKLY SYSTEMS

Week 1: check gearbox oil level; check plug for gap and condition.

Week 2: check brakes for adjustment, freedom and control action, and lubrication of cables; check wheels for security; rock wheels and front fork to check play in bearings; examine tyre treads and adjust pressures.

Week 3: examine all electrical leads for signs of abrasion or fracture; check all terminals for security; check operation of horn, lamps and dip-switch; check contact-breaker setting.

Week 4: check clutch cable for adjustment; check that clutch plates are freeing; check all nuts and bolts for security; check battery.

By employing the daily system, the rider ensures that most of the major

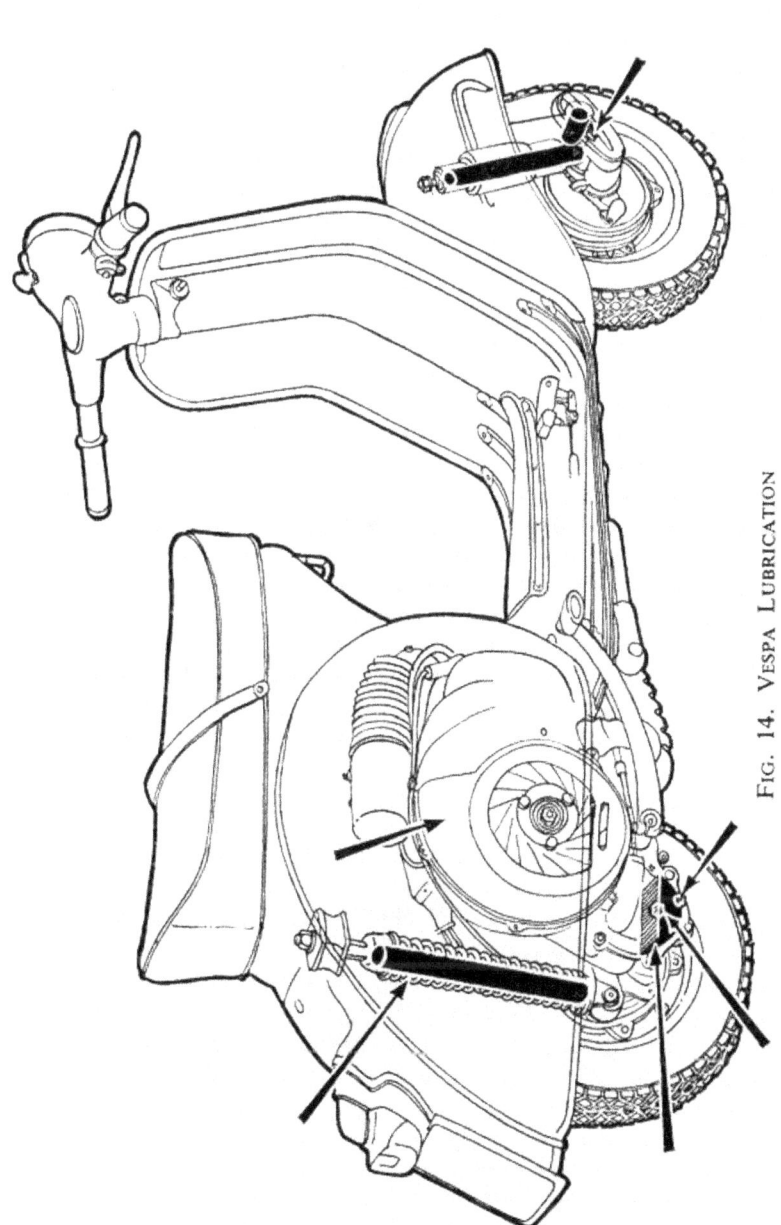

FIG. 14. VESPA LUBRICATION

These are the components which need lubrication. The dampers contain a special light hydraulic fluid; the bushing of the front suspension relies on greasing. The engine is fed with oil mixed with the petrol; and the gearbox oil also lubricates the inner main bearing. Arrowed on the gearbox are the drain and filler plugs. Parts such as the steering head and wheel bearings—and the outer main bearing—are pre-packed with grease.

points are checked at least once each week. Even allowing for a pretty substantial mileage each day this should mean, at the worst, that no fault could go undetected for more than, say, 300 miles. So, most defects would

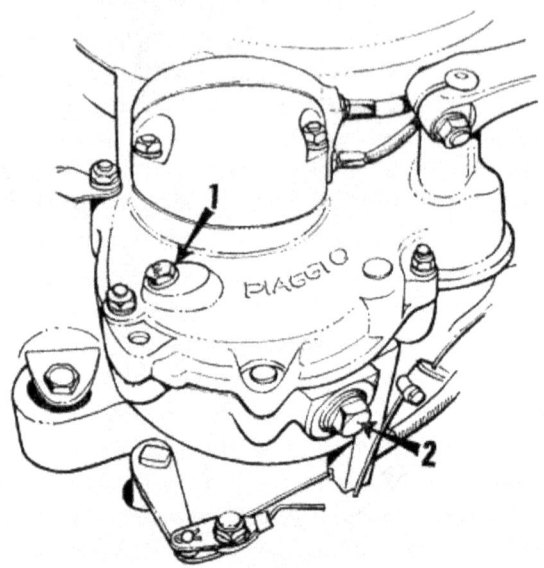

FIG. 15. THE GEARBOX PLUGS

Make sure that both these plugs are tight. No. 1 is the filler (its actual position varies on different models, as the Appendix explains). No. 2 is the drain plug, which is magnetic to attract swarf. Always drain the oil with the engine hot.

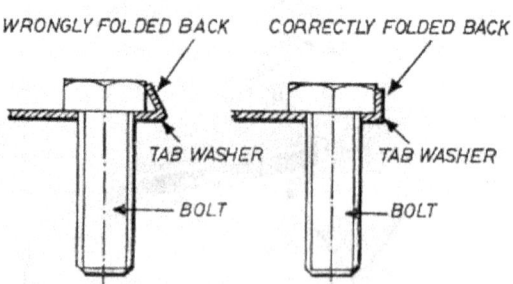

FIG. 16. SECURITY FOR BOLTS

Where tab washers are used, there are right and wrong ways of folding them back. The wrong way is on the left; the correct one on the right. Never omit washers—of any type—when rebuilding an engine.

be discovered well before they had time to develop to serious proportions.

With the weekly system, a month could elapse between the beginning of a fault and its discovery. Now, where the machine is used for only a 50-mile week-end jaunt this would be neither here nor there—but if the machine is used more frequently than this it's best to settle for the daily checks instead.

The important thing is to *check* the relevant points. In nine cases out of ten no adjustment will be necessary: you are only examining the component to find out if it needs to be touched, and where everything is in order you merely leave well alone and pass on to the next point on the list.

Neither system, however, takes into account periodic oil changing and greasing, which must still be carried out on the elapsed mileage basis recommended by the manufacturers and set out in the Appendix. And as it's all too easy to forget just when the job was last done, a useful aid to memory in this department is to stick a piece of self-adhesive tape to the parts concerned, noting on the tape the mileage at which the work was last done, or the mileage at which it should next be done.

A word of warning, here, about grades of oil and greases. The Appendix lists certain grades of lubricant which should be used. The manufacturers do not pick these names out of a hat; nor do they suggest them because they get a "rake-off" from the oil companies. They don't!

The factory and the research departments of the oil companies both carry out long and expensive tests with the various components, using a wide range of oils and greases. The brands which give the best results—longest life with the least friction—are the brands which are eventually recommended. So stick to them, and do not be tempted to use a different grade of lubricant because it is cheaper or because you have read in an advertisement that it has some magical properties. It may well have them, but unless they happen to be the right properties for your particular machine the results may not be as pleasant as you think.

CHAPTER FIVE

WORKING ON VESPA ENGINES

To those about to wed, the traditional advice is "Don't"—and to some extent that holds true, too, for those about to work on Vespa engine/gearbox units. They are not the easiest of mechanisms to strip, and without a great deal of background knowledge and a number of special tools there is a considerable danger that one will do more damage than good by attempting over-ambitious jobs.

That does not mean, of course, that one can do nothing. Decarbonizing, for example, is well within the range of the least mechanically-minded owner. The contact-breaker unit can be serviced, and the clutch stripped sufficiently for the plates to be renewed. Beyond that, however, it is inadvisable to go. Even main bearing renewal demands that the unit be split, and though it is possible to renew the small-end bush easily enough by means of an improvised puller, one then comes up against the problem that it must be reamed. Few scooterists' workshops include reamers in the tool kit, so here again you meet the hard realities.

Happily, of course, the Vespa unit very seldom calls for major work. The average owner is, therefore, most unlikely to be called upon to do more than the jobs mentioned above, coupled with tracing and rectifying any faults which develop in running. These, by their nature, are prone to be associated with ignition or carburation rather than with the mechanics.

In this section, therefore, I have confined myself to describing the work which everybody can do; and have not touched at all upon the more advanced jobs which call for the sure touch of a skilled mechanic. You will find the bones of them in the official Workshop Manuals.

DECARBONIZING

As we have seen, the whole basis of the scooter engine is that its fuel is burned in the combustion chamber. Naturally, there are by-products of this combustion, of which the chief is carbon. This is, in fact, a form of soot—a hardish deposit which over the miles, builds up, until it covers the piston crown; the inner faces of the combustion chamber; and the exhaust port. Carbon also forms in the exhaust pipe and in the silencer.

Naturally, the effect of this build-up is to reduce the effective size of the combustion chamber; to block the exhaust port, and so make it harder for burned gases to escape; and to choke the silencer. Inevitably, if the engine is left to its own devices the carbon will accumulate to such an extent that the motor will hardly run at all. But, long before then, its power will have been drastically reduced. Overheating and pinking may occur.

It is not so long ago since it was necessary to "decoke" a two-stroke every two or three thousand miles to keep it on the top line, and even now —despite advances in fuels and oils which have reduced carbon deposits dramatically—it will repay you to carry out this pretty simple job at intervals of no more than 5,000 miles. On the other hand, you *can* leave

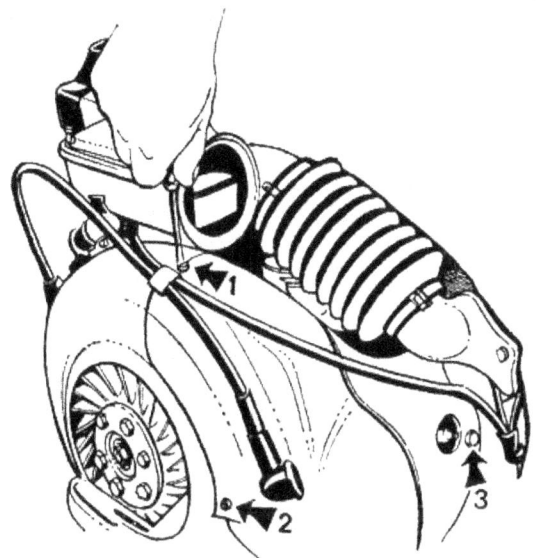

FIG. 17. DETACHING THE FAN COWL

There are three fastenings for the fan cowl, shown arrowed here. The air hose is detached after loosening the clip at the air filter end.

it two or even three times that mileage and get away with it; though by doing so you will probably cut the life of your engine. Douglas recommend that the job should be done at intervals of 4,800 miles. Piaggio themselves say 2,400 miles—Italian conditions, presumably, being harder on engines than ours.

Decarbonizing calls for the possession of a few simple tools and little else. You will need a screwdriver to remove the fan trunking; spanners for the sparking plug, the cylinder head, and the exhaust pipe and silencer. A scraper is necessary, but this can be improvised by filing a stick of solder until it is wedge-shaped, or by using a wedge-shaped piece of wood, or even by pressing into service a really blunt kitchen knife. You will also need a brush and some paraffin or grease solvent; a baking dish to use as a tray; a wire brush or some steel wool; a couple of old piston rings, one of them broken in half, and a supply of rag. As a general rule, one's stock of spares kept in the workshop should also include a set of gaskets and a spare set of piston rings—just in case of mishaps.

Preparatory work. Set the scooter on its stand and remove the engine cowl. Pull the plug lead from the sparking plug. Then insert a small screwdriver into the eye of the pin on the air cleaner hose clip, and turn it once or twice to loosen the grip on the hose. Then slide the end of the hose clear of the air cleaner, and undo the screws which hold the top cover of the cleaner to the carburettor. Lift the cleaner away, and remove the base screws on the fan cowling (*see* Fig. 17). Then undo the single bolt adjacent to the sparking plug hole, and take the cowl off the cylinder.

Examine the barrel. If it is dirty, give the outside of the engine a

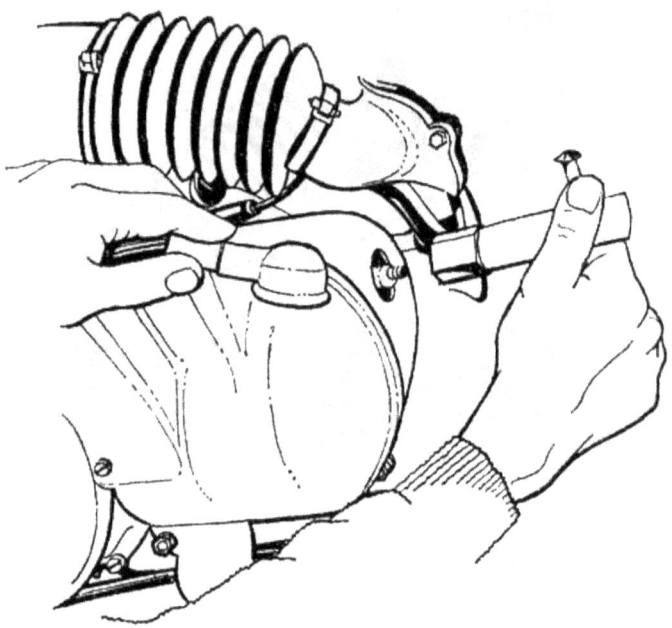

FIG. 18. SPARKING PLUG REMOVAL

The sparking plug is reached through a hole in the fan trunking, after pulling off the plug cap.

thorough brushing with paraffin or grease solvent before proceeding further. Under no circumstances must dirt be permitted to enter the engine. After brushing away all the grit, mop up with rag. Then remove the sparking plug (*see* Fig. 18). The main part of the job can then be tackled.

Removing the cylinder head. Four nuts hold the cylinder head to the barrel, and these must be detached after first loosening each one a few threads at a time, working from one to another, diagonally, across the head. Doing the job this way helps to reduce the stresses involved. When the nuts are off, slide the head away from the studs (*see* Figs. 19 and 20). If it sticks, don't under any circumstances attempt to lever it off by inserting a screwdriver or a rod into the joint. Instead, use a block of softwood as a "cushion." Butt one end of the block against the head and tap the other end gently with a hammer. This should rapidly break the joint. If that fails, replace the sparking plug and kick the engine over sharply. The force of compression should then lift the head for you.

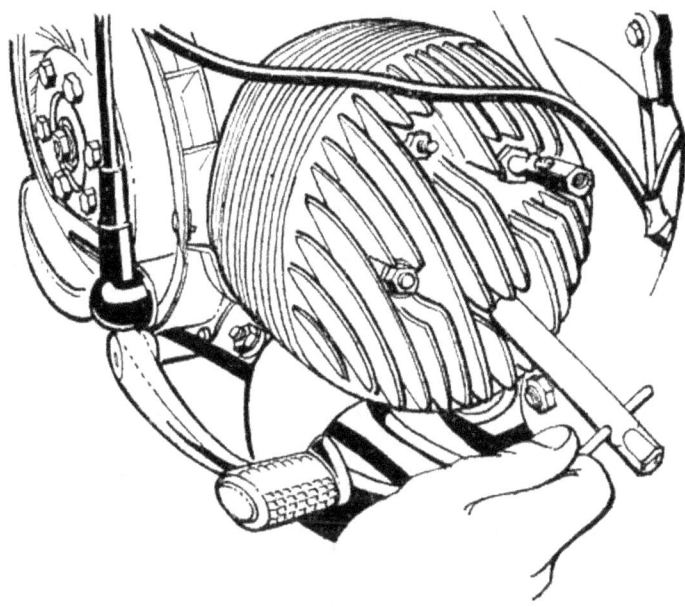

FIG. 19. HOW TO DECARBONIZE, 1

With the fan cowl and carburettor detached, undo the four head nuts. Note that the nut adjacent to the sparking plug is extended and tapped to provide a mounting for the fan cowl.

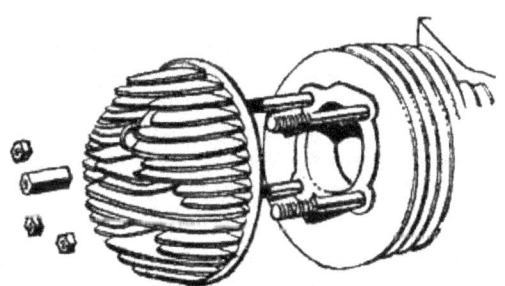

FIG. 20. HOW TO DECARBONIZE, 2

Lift out the head nuts, and slide the cylinder head off its studs. How to free a sticking head is described in the text.

It may be, however, that on an elderly engine there has been corrosion between the head and the studs. If so, give all the studs a liberal dosing with penetrating oil, and leave it to soak for some hours. Then try either of the two methods already recommended.

Access to the exhaust port. Where decarbonizing is carried out regularly there is usually no need to remove the barrel every time. Instead, all the necessary work can be done on the piston crown, the inside of the head, and through the open exhaust port.

Having removed the head, therefore, it is only necessary to undo the exhaust pipe clamping bolt and the silencer fastenings. Pull the exhaust system off the machine, and the way is clear for a top overhaul.

Work on the head. Start the decoke by chipping away as much carbon as possible from the cylinder head, making sure you don't score the actual metal. Take particular care when dealing with the area around the sparking plug hole, where carbon build-up can have particularly unhappy results. If the sparking plug threads themselves have collected carbon, pick it out—gently—by use of a large darning needle. But here, again, be very gentle. Don't let the steel point gouge into the soft metal of the head.

When all the carbon has been roughly scraped away, finish the job with the steel wool. Or, better still, use a rotary wire brush in an electric drill. In this case, make sure that the edge of the brush holder does not abrade the corners of the combustion chamber. Ultra-fastidious riders like to finish this part of the job with metal polish to obtain a really good surface which offers less "key" for future carbon formation. Where this is done, the head must be washed in petrol before refitting.

Work on the piston crown. Holding the barrel so that it cannot move, turn the engine by means of the starter or the flywheel until the piston is at the top of its stroke. Then remove all traces of carbon from it in just the same way as you did with the head.

Some mechanics prefer, however, to leave a ring of carbon round the edge of the piston, believing that this gives improved oil- and pressure-sealing properties. To do this you need an old piston ring. Take the piston a little way down the barrel, and insert the old ring into the barrel mouth. Then bring the piston back up the bore until it is butted against the ring. The old ring now forms a template. Simply scrape and polish away all the carbon you can see, as before. When you remove the ring, you will find that a neat edging of carbon is left round your piston (*see* Fig. 21).

Work on the exhaust port. Being careful, once again, not to allow the barrel to move, set the piston at T.D.C. and lightly smear the crown with grease. Vaseline will do nicely. Then take it right down the bore to the end of its stroke. By inserting a scraper from below, you can now clean out the exhaust port, any stray chips of carbon which enter the cylinder— and they will be very few—being neatly caught by the grease on the piston crown. When the port is free of all carbon give a few blasts through the barrel, from top to bottom, with a tyre pump.

With the barrel thus cleared, bring the piston back to the top of its stroke and wipe away the grease, complete with carbon chips.

WORKING ON VESPA ENGINES

Fuller decarbonizing. Although this "top" overhaul method is quite satisfactory after a moderate mileage, a high-mileage engine will require a fuller decoke to enable attention to be paid to the rings. This involves lifting the barrel and also removing the piston.

It can be done by tilting the engine while it is still attached to the frame, but it is often more convenient to remove it (see p. 43) and do

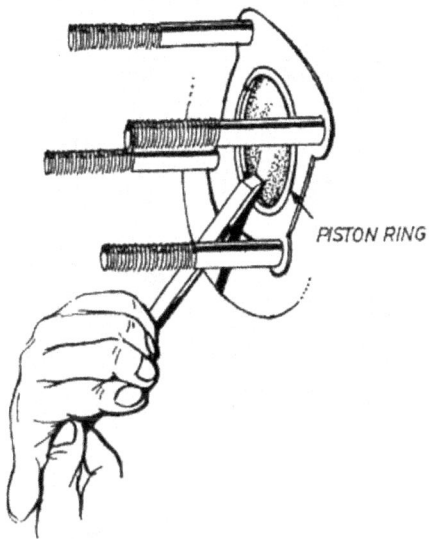

FIG. 21. How to Decarbonize, 3

Use a scraper to remove all carbon from the piston, save for a narrow ring round its outside edge. To protect this, insert an old piston ring as shown here.

the work on the bench. When stripping, follow the stages already described up to the removal of the head and the silencer. Then, gently draw the barrel off its studs—it may be necessary to free the nuts on the two front crankcase studs a little. Be careful to steady the piston as it emerges from the barrel, so that it does not fall down as the support of the bore is withdrawn.

Using circlip pliers, take out the gudgeon pin circlips. Then make a small mark on the piston crown so that you are sure which way round the piston should go and press out the gudgeon pin. If it is stiff, heat the piston by wrapping it in rag wrung out in hot water. After a minute or so, this should expand it sufficiently for the pin to be pushed out by hand pressure only (*see* Figs. 22 and 23).

You can now apply the full decarbonizing technique, which comprises all the work on the head, piston crown, and exhaust port already detailed —plus some extra jobs on the piston.

Cleaning the ring grooves. With the two thumbs, spring each ring in turn out of their grooves and lift them off the piston. Be careful not to bend the

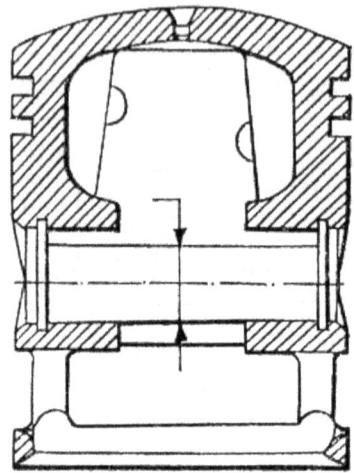

FIG. 22. THE PISTON IN CROSS SECTION

The gudgeon pin (arrowed) is located laterally in the piston by means of circlips. The grooves in which the piston rings fit must also be kept clear of carbon.

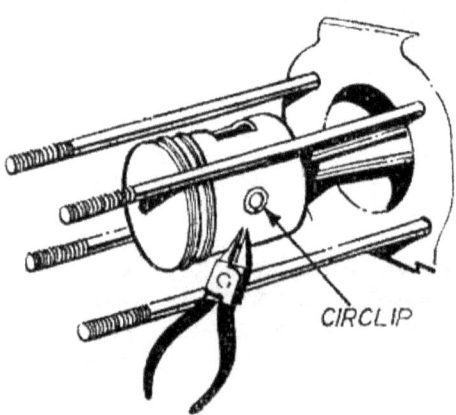

FIG. 23. REMOVING THE CIRCLIPS

To detach the piston, use a pair of pointed pliers to compress and pull out the circlips. Then heat the piston, as described in this chapter, and drive out the gudgeon pin. Note which way round the flat-top type of piston fits. The earlier deflector-type piston was set with the steep edge of the deflector upwards.

rings too much because they are made of brittle cast iron, and can easily snap. Place them on clean newspaper, top face uppermost, in the order of removal. This is very important, for each must go back into its original groove.

Now take an old ring, snapped into half, and use it as a scraper to clean all carbon out of the ring grooves (*see* Fig. 24). This is an essential job, for if the rings stick in their grooves they cannot provide a proper seal, and thus compression is lost. Finish the job off by *very gently* ridding the grooves of the last traces of carbon with a nail file.

Internal carbon. Next, use your scraper to get rid of any carbon which has formed on the inside of the piston. The crown, being hot in operation,

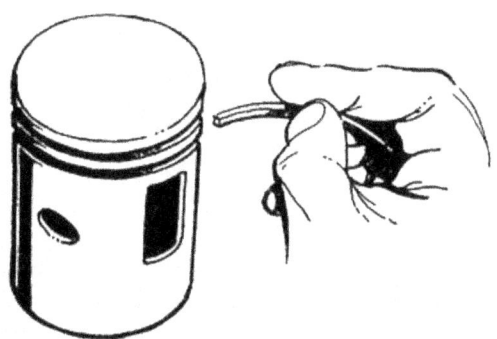

FIG. 24. CLEANING THE RING GROOVES
A piece of piston ring, broken off to form a miniature scraper, is the best tool for the job.

does tend to carbonize some of the crankcase oil on itself. Finally, wash the piston in petrol to get rid of any remaining carbon chips or dust, and turn your attention to the rings.

Cleaning the rings. If there was carbon in the ring grooves there will also be carbon on the rings. It will have formed on the upper and lower surfaces, and on the inner periphery, and can be removed by gently scraping and washing in petrol. But the emphasis is on "gentle," for rings are very vulnerable indeed.

Checking for wear. Having cleaned them thoroughly, check the rings for wear by inserting one at a time into its groove—open end outwards—and rolling it round (*see* Fig. 25) to ensure that it is a good fit. It must not be tight.

That done, test the gap by inserting each ring in turn into the barrel, about half an inch down from the top. Square it up with the piston—inserted from the other end—and use feeler gauges to measure the ring gap (*see* Fig. 26). On a used ring a maximum of 2 mm gap is permissible, and it should not be less than 0·2 mm on a new one. A tight ring can be opened up by cutting off the excess metal with an ultra-fine file; but a slack ring must be renewed.

Cleaning the silencer. It is not possible to open up a Vespa silencer for cleaning, and consequently these components have a "life" of only some 20,000 miles before there is a danger of serious clogging. Replacement with a new unit at this stage is always advisable.

One can, however, scrape away any carbon visible in the exhaust pipe

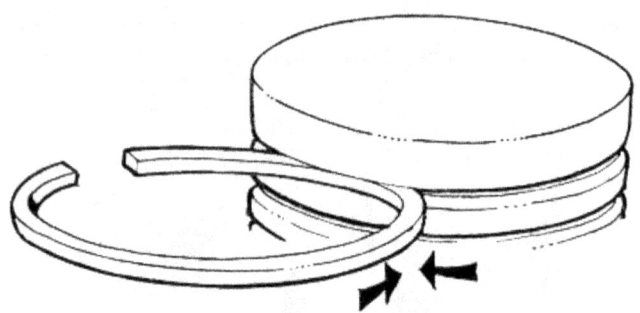

FIG. 25. CLEARANCE IN THE GROOVES

The rings can be checked for free fitting in their grooves by inserting each as shown, and rolling it round the piston. If there are tight spots the ring should be eased a little. This is best done with emery cloth laid on a face-plate.

and the tail pipe, and also take the unit to a garage and ask them to burn out as much carbon as possible with a blow lamp. At home, one can get rid of the worst of the accumulated carbon by immersing the silencer in a

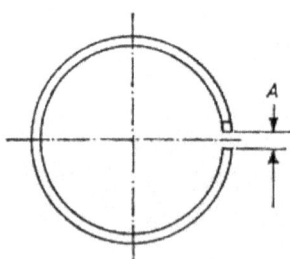

FIG. 26. PISTON RING GAP

The gap "A" should be, at the most, 2 mm. It is checked by setting the ring squarely in the bore, half an inch from the top, and inserting feeler gauges into the gap to measure it.

bath of hot caustic soda. This should be made up of three pounds of soda to a gallon of water—and it is corrosive, so keep it clear of your skin and eyes, and don't allow any light alloy to come into contact with it. If you do get any on yourself, wash it off at once with plenty of water.

After the silencer has had a good bath in this mixture—which will soften up the carbon—it should be well washed in slightly soapy warm water before refitting to the machine.

Rebuilding the engine. Fit the rings back on to the piston. The lower ring goes on first, and this is brought up from the skirt of the piston and set in its groove. Make sure that the ring engages properly on the ring peg. Then add the top ring, and make a similar check.

Heat the piston as before, and fit it to the connecting rod by means of the gudgeon pin. Spring the circlips back into position, and place the new cylinder base gasket—lightly oiled—on the crankcase mouth. Smear fresh engine oil round the cylinder walls, and slide the barrel back on to the studs. Feed the rings carefully into the mouth of the barrel, pressing each one so that it is fully compressed and does not catch the edge of the barrel as it slides in.

Refit the cylinder head, and the four washers for the head nuts. Take the nuts themselves up to finger tightness, and then use the spanner to give each a couple of turns at a time. Start with the lower right. Then go to the upper left, the upper right, and the lower left in that order. Keep tightening them in this way until they are properly locked down.

Next replace the silencer, tightening its clamp bolt thoroughly. Add the sparking plug—properly cleaned and gapped—and use a new copper-asbestos plug washer. This will cost only a few pence, but will ensure that the plug is compression-tight.

Replace the fan cowling; reconnect the air filter; and test the engine before putting back the cowling. If new rings have been fitted, run the machine gently for the first hundred miles or so to give them a chance to bed in.

Engine removal and stripping. As I have already indicated, removing and stripping an engine is really a job for a trained mechanic. However, the following general sequence can be applied to all G.S. models and can be used in emergency. Start by blocking up the machine with the rear wheel off the ground, and detach the wheel nuts and the brake drum screws. Then undo the axle centre nut. Free off the exhaust system, and all pipes, cables and electrical leads on the engine. Take off the air cleaner and its pipe, and undo the engine mountings on early models or the pivot bolts on later ones. The unit can then be lifted to the bench.

Remove the carburettor, the fan cowling, the head and barrel, and the cooling fan. Heat the piston, spring out the circlips, and drive out the gudgeon pin. Place a suitable drift through the small end, and slide a pair of wood blocks between this and the crankcase mouth to lock the crankshaft while the flywheel centre nut is undone. This will draw the flywheel off its shaft. Early models had a separate fan housing, which should be removed, followed by the stator plate. Before lifting this, scribe matching marks on the plate and the crankcase so that it can be refitted accurately.

Remove the starter pedal, and turn to the clutch side of the unit. Unbolt the clutch cover, remove the centralizing plate from the clutch body, and again lock the crankshaft with the wooden blocks. Undo the clutch nut, and draw the clutch off its shaft. This requires the use of an extractor

(Tool No. 0020111 on 160 c.c. and 180 c.c. machines; Tool No. 0020128 on 150 c.c. models).

To strip the clutch, a special compressor (T.0020322) is required (*see* Fig. 27). This compresses the springs so that the circlip in the rear edge of the clutch drum can be sprung out. A substitute tool can easily be fabricated from a coach bolt, tubular spacer, and a wing nut and washers.

To split the crankcase, release the crankcase and gearcase nuts and detach the gear index plate. Tap gently but smartly, all round the joint

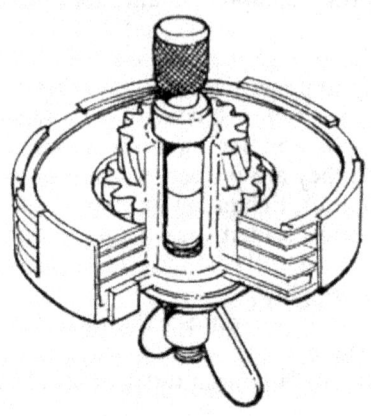

FIG. 27. DISMANTLING THE CLUTCH

The correct tool for dismantling the clutch after removal from the shaft is shown here. It compresses the springs and allows the circlip set round the inner side of the drum to be removed. A substitute is described in the text.

with a hide-faced mallet until the cases part. Have a tray underneath to catch the oil which is lost as this happens. Under no circumstances try to lever the cases apart with a screwdriver. This will have a two-fold result—a damaged joint and, probably, a cracked case. Persistent tapping with the mallet will eventually free the joint, so persevere with it.

When the cases part the fan side can be pulled off, leaving the crankshaft and gears in the clutch side. The fan side bearing can be removed after detaching the circlip and heating the case to 80° C. The same procedure should be used to fit a new bearing, which must be prepacked with grease. Rebuilding is simply a reversal of this procedure.

THE FUEL SYSTEM

Filler cap. If the vent hole in the filler cap is blocked, fuel starvation will occur. The reason is simple. If air cannot enter the tank the result is to set up a suction, which prevents fuel leaving it. In all cases of intermittent firing, check that the vent hole is clear by poking through it with a piece of thin wire.

WORKING ON VESPA ENGINES

Carburettor cleaning. All the later Vespa G.S. machines are fitted with a carburettor which has a "guillotine" throttle slide, but which is outwardly similar to the normal needle-valve type of instrument. It is, however, somewhat more sophisticated, being equipped with an air corrector jet and a starter system which is far less "fundamental" than the old-type air strangler.

The only adjustments which are possible with this type of carburettor are to the idling setting; and generally speaking it is better to let well alone.

FIG. 28. AIR FILTER REMOVAL

Access to the air-filter element is gained by removing the top of the filter casing, as shown. The element itself is seated in the lower section of the case.

Once a year, however, the instrument should be removed from the scooter for cleaning. This involves releasing the throttle cable, removing the air filter (*see* Fig. 28), detaching the fuel pipe, and undoing the nuts which hold the carburettor to the induction flange. When the carburettor has been lifted off, stuff clean rag into the flange so that no dirt can enter the crankcase.

Cleaning should be done with petrol and a clean stiff-bristled brush. First, wipe the entire outside with petrol-soaked rag to get rid of any grit. Then remove the filter cover, take out the filter gauze, and swill both this and the filter chamber with clean petrol. Next, take off the float chamber top and clean out any dirt which has accumulated in it. You will need to test the float and the needle valve, too. Try shaking the float close to your ear. If you hear liquid swilling around in it, then you have a puncture and you should fit a new float. If the machine has covered upwards of 15,000 miles it is a good scheme, as a general rule, to completely renew the needle valve and all the jets. The reason is that petrol is not clinically pure. It almost invariably contains *some* grit, however fine. In time, this wears the surfaces of the valve and the jets and they lose their original pin-point accuracy.

So, screw out these components—one at a time, so that you know exactly which has come from where—and either clean them in petrol if the mileage is under 15,000; or fit the new part in the place of each one as it is removed where the machine is over the limit. You can see the location of the various parts on the accompanying illustrations.

The older 150 c.c. G.S. models, of course, have the needle-jet carburettor. Here, the procedure is still virtually the same, save that renewals should include the slide, the needle, and the needle jet itself. All of these tend to wear in use, and upset the carburation.

When rebuilding a carburettor, note that the gaskets should invariably be replaced "dry," using neither jointing compound nor oil. The reason is simple. If these are used, a proportion of it is likely to be squeezed into the instrument as the screws are tightened, and jet blockage may result.

Where a jet has become blocked, do not be tempted to push a needle or a length of wire through it in an attempt to clean it out. All you will do is to damage the soft metal of the jet instead. You *can* use a clean bristle from a brush; but usually a jet can be cleared by blowing hard through it from the direction opposite to that in which the fuel normally flows.

Setting the idling. First, warm up the engine. Then screw the throttle stop screw in until a fast idle is obtained. Fully screw in the slow running regulation screw—not absolutely tight, or you may damage its metering face, and then undo it one and a half turns. Restart the engine, and slow the idling down to normal by loosening the throttle screw. Snap the throttle open, and note if the engine picks up immediately. If it hesitates or stalls, richen the idling mixture a little by screwing the air regulation screw in by a quarter turn. Then try again. If, on the other hand, it does not stall, unscrew the regulator by a quarter turn. The aim is to obtain the weakest mixture which will permit even idling and a clean pick-up.

When this has been obtained—and it should take only a very little experiment to obtain the correct setting—reduce the idling speed to normal by means of the throttle stop screw.

CHAPTER SIX

LOOKING AFTER THE ELECTRICS

You can regard the electrical system of your Vespa as a generating station and distribution system in miniature—which is just what it is. As such, it is a quite remarkable example of design for a purpose—simple, strong, and very reliable providing it is given the minimum of attention required.

Contact-breaker points adjustment. On the ignition side, this is perhaps the most important single adjustment you need to make. To some extent,

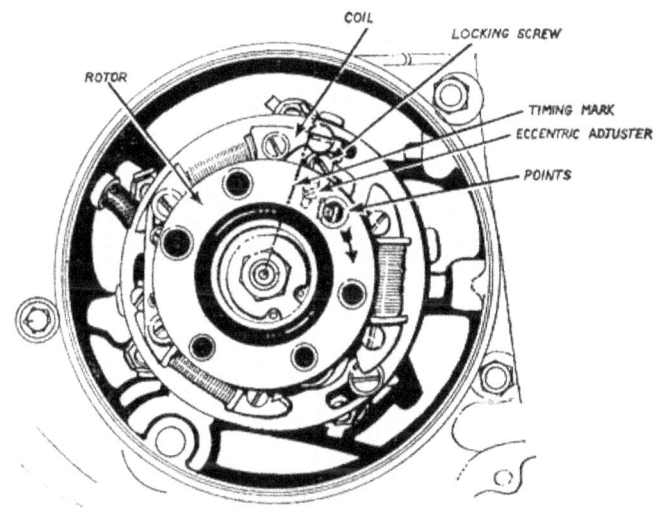

Fig. 29. The Contact-Breaker Points
With the flywheel removed, but the rotor still in place, this is how the contact-breaker points look for adjustment. Clean contacts and check adjustment every 5,000 miles.

the contact-breaker setting controls the timing of the spark, and an incorrect adjustment can seriously interfere with the performance of the machine.

The points are mounted on the stator plate and are actuated by a cam on the main shaft. They are accessible for adjustment either through slots in the flywheel face, on some of the earlier models, or by removing the flywheel itself on later ones (*see* Fig. 29).

Where the flywheel has to be detached, first gear should be engaged and the engine cowl removed. With the machine off its stand, the flywheel centre nut should then be undone. If you have a helper to sit aboard and keep the brakes on it will make this part of the job easier.

Next, remove the sparking plug and disengage gear. Now turn the engine over until the points are observed to be fully open. To be absolutely sure about this, it helps if you insert a small slip of white paper behind them. A cigarette paper is ideal. You can then see at a glance whether or not they are open properly, moving the shaft back and forth a little until you have the points in such a position that shifting the shaft either way will start to close them.

Now, measure the gap. It should be no less than 0·3 mm (0·011-in.) and no more than 0·5 mm (0·019-in.). If it falls outside these limits it will need to be adjusted. This is done by slackening the screw which you will find just above the points. Do not undo this fully. It is enough if you loosen it by a couple of turns. Then insert your feeler gauge—use the 0·4 mm (0·015-in.) blade between the points—and turn the eccentric adjusting screw (the small one, just below the points) until you can just, and only just, move the feeler in and out. Tightening the adjuster screw even a little more should cause the points to grip the blade and hold it absolutely immovable. Retighten the locking screw and your points are set.

Or are they? When you are dealing with clearances as small as this, even the action of tightening the screw can disturb the setting. So, after locking it down you should recheck. Do this, first, by trying to insert the 0·5 mm (0·019-in.) blade. It should not fit. If it does, try using the 0·6 mm blade (0·021-in.). If *that* enters then your points setting has opened up outside the permissible limits and you will have to do the job again. If it jibs at the 0·6 mm blade, all is well.

Where neither of the larger blades will fit, try the 0·4 mm one. If that won't enter, drop down to 0·3 mm (0·011-in.). This, again, represents your lower limit. If it can't be inserted then you will need to re-adjust, because the gap is too small. All this quibbling about tenths of a millimetre may sound petty, but unless that setting is dead right then you are going to lose power and put up your fuel consumption.

Once you are absolutely certain about the accuracy of the adjustment, refit the flywheel (or, on older machines) replace the flywheel cover.

Cleaning the points. Contact-breaker points don't simply need to be properly set. They must be clean as well. Whenever one resets them, therefore, it is advisable to check on their cleanliness. There is a very simple way of ridding them of dirt. Tear off two or three strips of fairly stiff white paper, about three inches long and a quarter of an inch wide. Open the points, and insert a paper strip between them. Then turn the flywheel until the points are lightly gripping the paper and give it a sharp tug to withdraw it. In all probability it will come out soiled with dirt. Turn it round, insert the other end, and repeat the performance. Eventually, after several such operations, the paper strip will emerge clean and your points are fit for further service.

Replacing points. Providing the points are meeting squarely there is no need to do more than keep them clean. Eventually, however, they wear. The slight arcing of current which is almost bound to occur in use eats into the metal faces, pitting them and detracting from the contact-breaker's efficiency.

You can, of course, remove the contact-breaker and carefully grind the contact faces flat on a stone. Alternatively, your garage will probably have a points refacing machine which will do the job for you. On the other hand, the cost of a brand-new set is so small—and the job they do so important—that neither course is really worthwhile. If, on inspection, you find that the two points do not meet squarely and that the faces are pitted, then simply take them out and fit a new set.

Removal is extremely simple. The moving arm is held to its post by a spring circlip. Ease this off, and remove the clamp bolt holding the free end of the return spring on the contact-breaker arm. But, be very careful to note the disposition of the insulating washers on this bolt and below the moving arm. These *must* go back in the correct order, or you will have a short-circuited contact-breaker and no spark!

When you have taken off the moving arm, free the clamp bolt holding the fixed point plate, and draw it off the stator. Fit the new parts, and gap the points. Take the opportunity, also, of greasing the felt pad which lubricates the cam. Neglect of this simple job often leads to wear of the fibre arm, and consequent malfunctioning of the contact-breaker. Use a smear of the recommended high melting-point grease. This job should be done at 4,000-mile intervals. On early models, which had only face slots, use a light oil injected from an oil can, and be careful not to saturate the felt so much that lubricant is spread on to other components. It is sufficient to moisten the pad.

Demagnetization. This is a puzzling fault which, unfortunately, has no cure save to renovate the parts. The magnets in the flywheel lose their potency, usually because of work being carried out on the handlebar switch without the battery first being disconnected, or through the leads being connected in the reverse order to normal. Take the parts to a dealer for attention.

Retiming the ignition. The best way to retime Vespa ignition is to use a timing disc—a cheap cardboard one will do very well. Remove the flywheel, but leave the rotor in place, by undoing the three screws on the flywheel boss while leaving the centre nut tight. Fix the timing disc to the rotor in such a way that when the piston is at T.D.C., zero degrees on the disc is lined up with an improvised pointer fixed to any convenient part of the unit. Then turn the engine against the direction of rotation until the pointer indicates 26° *before* T.D.C., plus or minus one degree. At this point the contacts should just be opening. If they are not, loosen the clamping screw and reset them. Then check that the maximum gap is 0·5 mm (0·019-in.) in the normal way.

Ignition timing (Super Sports models only). Remove the six securing bolts and extract the rotor from the central hub. Then take out the plug, and engage neutral. Turn the hub by hand until the line which is scribed on it coincides with the extreme right-hand edge of the H.T. feed coil. At this point the contact-breaker points should be just opening. If this is so, turn the rotor until the points are fully open and check that they are within the correct limits of 0·3–0·5 mm (0·011–0·019-in.).

Where adjustment of the timing is necessary, re-align the scribed line with the coil and slacken the three screws which hold the stator plate to the crankcase. Then turn the plate anti-clockwise to advance the timing; clockwise to retard it.

Care of the battery. Several different types of battery are used on scooters —the "dry" battery, in which the electrolyte is in jelly form and the "wet" battery which contains a liquid electrolyte. The dry-type battery—the S.A.F.A.-Varley—is topped up after a journey has been completed by the simple expedient of adding a teaspoonful of distilled water to each cell. After the battery has been allowed to stand for a quarter of an hour all excess moisture is removed, either by siphoning or by shaking it out. When a battery of this type is to be recharged it must be topped up with distilled water both before and during charging. This must be at a rate of 0·75 amps and must continue for 24 hours. At the end of that time, the excess moisture is, again, either siphoned out or shaken away.

"Wet" batteries need to be inspected from time to time to ensure that the electrolyte level is still correct. It should be just above the plates inside each cell, and where it is not, enough distilled water should be added to bring it up to this level. One does not, by the way, add any form of acid— only distilled water. One does not use tap water, either, for this contains impurities which may, through chemical action, cut the life of the battery. However, as running with too low an electrolyte level can result in buckled plates and a ruined battery one must use a certain amount of discrimination in this matter. If the choice is to use a battery which is badly down, or else add something other than distilled water, then the lesser of the two evils is to use tap water. A better emergency stand-by, however, is water obtained from defrosting a refrigerator (or melting some of the ice accumulated on the freezer compartment). At a pinch, even well-boiled and cooled rainwater filtered through a nylon stocking will do. The best bet, however, is to keep a small bottle of distilled water handy. A chemist will supply a whole pint for sixpence or so, so the investment is hardly a crippling one!

The specific gravity must be checked monthly. This is done by using a hydrometer to take a sample from each cell. The hydrometer float will indicate certain readings, of which 1·270 to 1·290 (at 60° F) shows that the cell is fully charged. If any of the cells is significantly down on this figure —a relative term, since a fully discharged battery will register just a little over 1·1—then you must take the battery to a garage for recharging.

One further point. Battery terminals *must* be kept clean. If there is an accumulation of corrosion salts on them—or even if they are oxidized—they cannot do their job properly. Corrosion can be neutralized by applying a moderately strong solution of bicarbonate of soda. Oxidization can be removed by energetic wire brushing. When the terminals are clean, protect them by applying a liberal coating of Vaseline or lanolin.

Care of the switches. The switches are the only other "mechanical" parts of the electrical system. They require little attention apart from being opened up once a year for the terminals to be examined for security and the metal for signs of oxidization. The spring which controls the tumbler should also be given a little light oil—not enough to contaminate the terminals—so that the smooth action of the switches is maintained and the risk of selecting a "neutral" between any of the switch positions is eliminated.

Care of the loom. The wiring harness is tough and well protected, and only sheer bad luck or sheer bad maintenance will cause it any damage. However, it should be checked at regular intervals for signs of cut insulation or faulty terminals. If repairs have to be made to a lead it is always best to plait the conductors together and then run in a little solder to make the joint permanent. "Joints" which consists of wires twisted together rapidly oxidize and set up a high resistance. After repairs, wrap two or three turns of insulating tape round the affected area.

Care of the bulbs. Bulbs do not last for ever—nor are they designed to do so—but the average scooter headlamp bulb should give up to 1,500 hours of use if it is not maltreated.

The main thing is to ensure that the bulb is in good electrical contact at all times. This means that the holder—and the bulb cap—must both be kept bright and clean where they touch each other, since dirt causes a high electrical resistance. The same applies to the lamp and bulb terminals. Buff all contact surfaces with wire wool, and where the lamp terminal is spring-loaded give the spring a little light oil to ensure that it holds the terminals in good contact.

It pays to check the bulbs before each winter begins, and to replace any whose envelopes show signs of darkening. Filaments can be tested by holding the bulb in one hand, and flicking one's fingers at it. If the filament is weak it will collapse under even this light impact. That is not—as it may seem—the waste of a bulb. It eliminates a potential source of inconvenience—and perhaps of danger—on the road.

Always carry spare bulbs with you. If, on coming to replace a bulb, you find that it has seized in its holder you can usually remove it without danger to your fingers by wrapping insulating tape round the glass envelope first. Where this has happened, the interior of the bulb holder should be cleaned thoroughly with steel wool as soon as possible, since it is efficient neither electrically nor mechanically.

Care of lenses and reflectors. The power of a lamp depends mainly upon its lens and its reflector. The reflector concentrates the rays of light from the bulb and directs them into a penetrating beam instead of allowing them to scatter in all directions. The lens is designed to control this beam so that the best possible light pattern is obtained. If a lens has been broken, therefore, it must be replaced as soon as possible by one of the correct pattern. And where the reflector has become rusted this, too, must be renewed. You cannot polish reflectors—they are silvered, not chromed —and "penny wise, pound foolish" expedia such as lining the reflector with strips of chrome tape—excellent as a "get you home" device if you *are* caught out with a tarnished reflector—are not satisfactory as a permanent repair.

CHAPTER SEVEN

BRAKES, TYRES AND FORKS

THANKS to the constant development which the Vespa has undergone there is virtually nothing to do on the running gear of the machine, save to carry out the routine adjustments to the brake, throttle, clutch and gear control cables.

The rider's subconscious tendency to accept the gradual deterioration in braking power as the linings wear has been mentioned earlier. So, too, has the need to carry out regular checks on the brake adjustment to combat this.

Both front and rear brakes are adjusted by varying the relative lengths of the inner and outer control cables. For the front brake, the screw-type

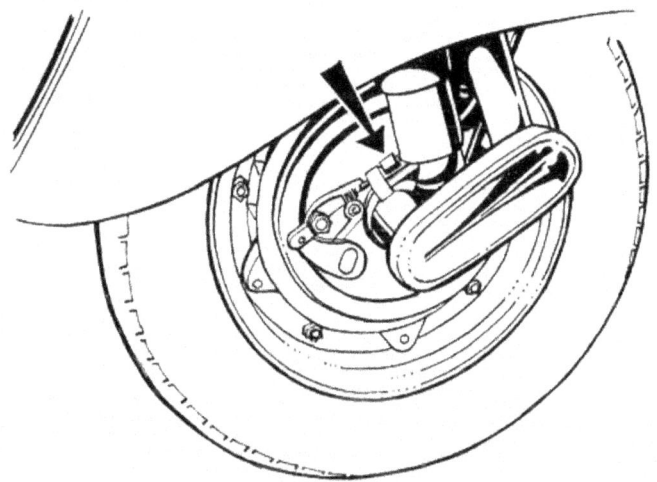

FIG. 30. FRONT BRAKE ADJUSTMENT

This adjuster is used in the same way as that on the rear brake. As the front brake takes a major share of the braking effort, it pays to get the settings absolutely right.

adjuster, with lock-nut, is fitted on the brake plate itself. The rear brake adjuster is screwed into an abutment on the engine casing. In both cases, the lock-nut is loosened, and the adjuster is racked out until the brake is just binding and preventing the wheel from turning. At this point, the adjuster is released slightly and the wheel turned again. The adjustment is correct when the wheel can turn freely. So set, the brake will come on with the minimum of movement of its lever or pedal. The lock-nut is then tightened to hold the adjustment (*see* Figs. 30 and 31).

When no further adjustment remains the brake drums must be removed, and the brake-shoes eased from their pivots, against which they are spring loaded. Service exchange brake-shoes, which are ready lined, should be substituted for them. This is a better method altogether than attempting to reline the existing shoes. Before replacing the brake drums give the working surfaces a wipe with clean rag, and rid them of any dust which has accumulated. Drums which have become scored or which have a noticeable degree of ovality—characterized by an "on-off-on" sensation

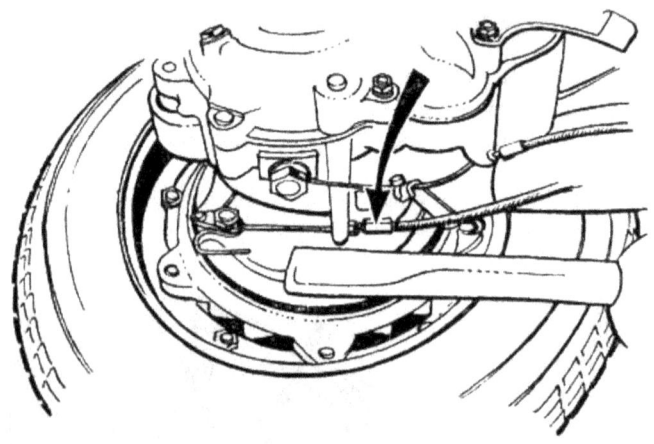

FIG. 31. REAR BRAKE ADJUSTMENT

Wear in the brake shoes is compensated by racking out this adjuster, so rotating the brake arm slightly and bringing the shoes nearer the drum. Before doing so, loosen its lock nut. After adjustment, retighten the lock nut so that the adjuster cannot vibrate loose.

when the brake is applied—must either be exchanged or taken to an engineering shop for truing and skimming.

When refitting or adjusting a front-brake cable it is essential to see that a good loop of cable is left between the point at which the cable emerges from the base of the steering column and the operating lever on the hub. If there is insufficient slack at this point the action of the front suspension can cause the brake to be continually applied and released. So, before assuming a fault in the brake drum, ensure that the cable control itself is not the culprit.

It is important, too, to remember that the control levers and the brake cam spindles must be lubricated periodically. If this job is neglected there is a danger that the parts may seize. Sticky operation of the brakes could almost certainly be attributed to insufficient attention to the lubrication of the cam pivots.

Breakage of the gear-change cables can often be traced to faulty assembly at the ferrule end. The twin cables are led through slots in the claws of the gear shifter, movement of the cables being transmitted to the claws by a ferrule screwed to each cable. Each ferrule has a hexagonal head, and if this should foul the edge of the claw the result is to allow the ferrule to turn with the claw, instead of revolving slightly. This results in bending of the cable and, eventually, in its failure through fatigue. Check this point when adjusting the gear control, and examine the edges of the claws for rough spots which would cause the ferrules to turn. If any are found, relieve them with a fine file.

A very fine clearance is specified for the adjustment of the clutch cable

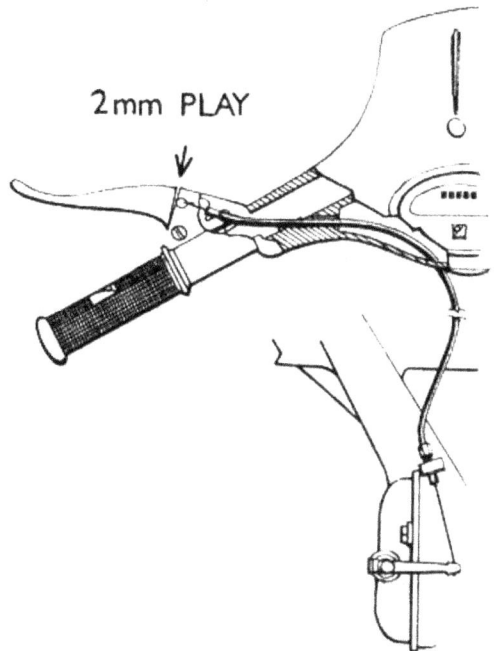

FIG. 32. CLUTCH ADJUSTMENT

The clutch control on the handlebar is linked to the clutch by means of a cable, and the adjuster is at the clutch end. It should be set so that the clutch lever has the amount of free play shown here before it starts to operate the mechanism.

on the Vespa. As with most two-wheelers, this is given as free play at the handlebar end, and is measured between the edge of the lever and its abutment on the bars (*see* Fig. 32). If smooth gear-changing is to be obtained from the machine, only two millimetres of play is permissible. This calls for care in the use of the adjuster, since it is equally impermissible to have the adjuster set so that no play at all is present. This can lead to clutch slip, and to burning of the clutch plates.

The plates can also be damaged if the gearbox oil level is allowed to drop below the specified mark. The clutch and gearbox depend upon the same supply for their lubrication, but owing to the relatively high position of the clutch a low oil level will not provide it with the oil it needs. The cork inserts will therefore tend to dry out and, after that, to burn. When this happens considerable damage can be done.

Tyres, being non-mechanical, are often badly overlooked. However, they require maintenance just as much as any other part of the machine. The pressure at which a tyre is run is all-important. If it is run soft, the sidewalls are subjected to bending loads, and continually flex. In time, they will crack and the tyre will be ruined. If, on the other hand, the tyre is pumped up too hard there is a danger that sudden contact with a stone or a hole in the road will induce such a high momentary compression of

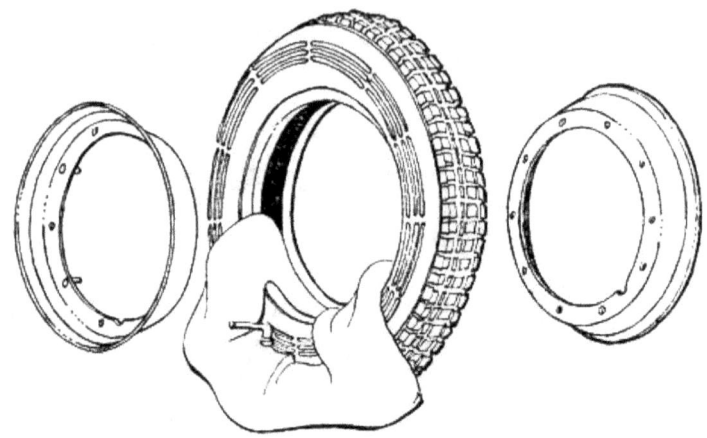

FIG. 33. VESPA SPLIT-RIM WHEELS

This is how the Vespa wheel comes apart for puncture repairs. It is essential to ensure that the seating areas for the tyre beads are clean and that the tyre itself is undamaged.

the air in the tyre that the tyre will burst. Hence the importance of maintaining the recommended pressures at all times, and of increasing the pressure in the rear tyre when a passenger is carried.

The tyre treads should be examined weekly, and any stones trapped in the grooves should be carefully eased out. Many of the stones which a tyre picks up are sharp flints. Each time the tyre revolves the road surface presses on them and drives them a little farther into the rubber, rather like a nail being hammered through the tread. If left undisturbed, such stones can eventually pierce the tread and the casing and cause a blow-out of the tube. At the least, they reduce the life of the tyre, so the few minutes spent on this job are amply repaid by obtaining a better mileage from the tyre.

When inflating a tyre, it is also important to make sure that the dust cap is put back on its valve. The cap serves a dual purpose: it prevents dirt from entering and possibly jamming the valve, and it is itself an efficient seal which will keep the pressure in the tyre even if the valve leaks.

If the tyre is left undisturbed for a long period there is a chance that it may bond itself to the metal of the wheel rims. If this happens the tyre has to be sacrificed by being cut from the rim. Again, though there is no cure, it is easy enough to prevent this happening. Periodically, remove the wheel, deflate the tyre, and release the bolts holding the split rim together (*see* Fig. 33). Detach the rims, and clean the bead seats thoroughly. Take out the tube, brush away any dirt which you find trapped in the case, and then liberally dust the tube and the tyre beads with French chalk before replacing them on the wheel rims.

For the rest, maintenance of the Vespa running gear entails nothing more complicated than keeping a watchful eye for loose nuts and bolts: adhering to the greasing and general lubrication routine; and cleaning the paintwork and chromium plating.

CHAPTER EIGHT

IF IT STOPS....

WHEN a doctor wishes to diagnose a patient's illness he works methodically, listing the various symptoms to build up an overall picture of the complaint. This done, he can identify it and give treatment accordingly.

Exactly the same type of diagnosis has to be made if a scooter engine refuses to work. Obviously there is a fault—some reason why the engine will not work—and before it can be cured it must first be located and identified. The search for it must be just as methodical as is the doctor's approach.

If certain requirements are being fulfilled then the engine *must* work. If it is not working, then it follows that one—or more—of these requirements is not being met, and fault tracing boils down to discovering which it is, and why it is not being supplied.

An engine *must* work if the correct charge of fuel-air mixture is being induced into the crankcase, transferred to the cylinder, properly compressed, fired at the right moment, and the residue properly exhausted. Only an obvious mechanical failure could otherwise stop the unit.

Consequently, fault tracing should always begin with an investigation into these five main requirements, and logically it would start with checking the petrol supply by peering into the tank to see that, in fact, there is a supply of fuel available. The next step should then be the equally obvious one of checking that the fuel is turned on and, if the tank level is low, that it is turned to the reserve position.

Once assured that the tank does contain fuel and that the tap is correctly set, the next check on the list is to ascertain whether or not the fuel is reaching the carburettor. It could be prevented by a blockage in the tap, by a blockage in the pipe, by an air lock, by a chocked filter, or by a jammed needle valve.

Normally, this initial check will have taken only a minute or so to carry out, but it will have given one of two quite definite answers. Either fuel is reaching the carburettor, or it is not. If it is not, then you have found at least a contributory cause of the trouble, and this should be rectified before proceeding. If it is reaching the carburettor, you can pass on to the next stage which, with a two-stroke, must always be to check the sparking plug, especially if carburettor flooding has occurred.

Where the engine has been badly overflooded, neat fuel will be trapped in the crankcase and there will be no chance of starting. Take out the plug, drain all fuel from the float chamber, and switch off the petrol. Then open the throttle wide, so that you admit as much air as possible, and turn the unit over on the kick-starter, briskly, about a dozen times. This should eject most of the trapped fuel. If the plug is wet, dry it; if necessary, burn the petroil off by holding the plug in the flame of a cigarette lighter or a match, and then replace it. Connect the H.T. lead, and operate the kick-starter. If the engine then fires, turn on the fuel. If it does not, turn on the fuel, allow a few seconds for the float chamber to fill, and then kick it again. It should then work satisfactorily.

If the initial inspection of the fuel system has brought no obvious fault to light, the next stage of the fault tracing should be switched to the ignition system. This is always a strong suspect with two-strokes, which tend to be very touchy indeed about their sparking plugs. So, first of all, remove the plug and examine the gap. Obviously this gap should be clear, but two-strokes can suffer from a condition called "whiskering."

Under the influence of heat, metallic particles contained in the fuel tend to weld themselves to the plug electrodes, until they eventually bridge the gap completely. When this happens, of course, no spark occurs, since the high-tension current can follow the easier path to earth provided by the whisker joining the electrodes. A whisker is cleared simply by flicking it away with the blade of a penknife or with a feeler gauge. At at pinch, a piece of thin cardboard or a folded piece of paper will suffice. Then give the plug a clean with a wire brush and regap it before replacing it. Persistent whiskering is a sign that something else is wrong, too. It can indicate that the wrong grade of plug is fitted, or that the engine is running too hot. This, in turn, points to poor scavenging or a weak mixture, and should suggest that either the exhaust system is becoming choked, or that a joint is leaking.

Where inspection of the plug shows the spark gap to be clear and neither over-wide nor too narrow, connect the plug to the H.T. lead and place its metal body in contact with the cylinder. Arrange matters so that you can easily see the gap while operating the kick-starter, and then turn the motor over smartly. A good fat spark should jump across the plug points. Repeat the check several times, and if no spark is obtained substitute a brand-new plug—an essential "spare" which should always be carried—and try again. If the new plug sparks and the old one didn't, the obvious inference is that the plug insulation has broken down, and fitting the new plug in its place should cure the trouble.

If no spark is obtained with the new plug, however, then the trouble lies somewhere between the sparking-plug terminal and the magneto, and a more exhaustive examination will have to be made.

Examine the H.T. lead minutely throughout its length, checking the terminals and inspecting the insulation for signs of cracks or perished areas which could be leading to a short-circuit. If you are doubtful about it, try the effect of substituting a spare length of H.T. lead and retesting with that. Examine all the electrical connexions on the H.T. and L.T. side of the machine.

Finally, remove the inspection plate or the flywheel and take a look at the contact-breaker points. Open them fully, and see if they are worn or dirty. Clean them by inserting a clean slip of card, close the points lightly on it, and withdraw it against their pressure. Do this two or three times, until the card comes away clean and dry. Then open the points fully again and check the gap with a feeler gauge. If everything seems to be in order you have then done all that is possible on the electrical side, so far as roadside checking is concerned. A full ignition test is a garage job.

Complete engine failure for any other cause is unlikely, except in the event of the piston rings being broken following a seizure. Other troubles are more likely to show in reduced performance or in erratic running.

One of the likelier causes of a lack of pulling power, for instance, is loss of compression, and it is possible, where this is suspected, to deduce where the fault lies from the way the engine behaves. If the crankcase seals have failed there will be a tendency for the unit to spit back through the carburettor, since extra air will be induced into the crankcase, thus weakening the mixture. Where the head joint is damaged—possibly the gasket on US 1 models—a characteristic hissing noise may be heard as gas is driven through the gap. In both cases the unit will tend to run hot and this, in turn, aggravates the trouble.

Following a seizure, as we have noted, the rings may have fractured. Or, on an engine which has not been decarbonized regularly, the rings may have "gummed up" in their grooves. This not only reduces both crankcase and cylinder compressions, but it also allows oil to be driven from the case into the cylinder. This oil burns, and the resulting smoke issuing from the tail pipe is a good clue to watch for. If at any time you have partially seized your engine, and immediately afterwards it loses performance and begins to smoke, the only wise course is to stop immediately. The rings have almost certainly been damaged, and any further running could seriously damage the bore, too. This is especially the case where a ring has broken, for its sharp edges will act as highly efficient cutting tools, and the cylinder can be ruined.

One puzzling fault is pre-ignition. The engine "pinks" continually—a metallic tinkling sound—and will even continue to run when the ignition is cut. This is caused by carbon deposits or a small sliver of metal in the head becoming red hot and igniting the mixture before the spark occurs. The cure is to decarbonize as soon as you possibly can.

Exactly the same process of elimination has to be followed when tracing faults in the lighting system. Faced with electricity, of course, most laymen simply give it best first time, but in fact electrical work is reasonably straightforward provided that magic word "circuit" is borne in mind. Circuits are the key to electricity. If electricity is present and the circuit is complete then the current *must* flow through it. If electricity is present but is not flowing then it follows that the circuit is not complete.

Faulty circuits are of two types—the open-circuit and the short-circuit. In the first case there is a complete break and the wires on the side of the breakage remote from the electrical source are "dead." In the case of a short-circuit the current is still flowing, but is following a shorter path to earth, as would happen, for instance, if one end of a live lead had become detached from its terminal and had earthed itself on the bodywork.

Obviously, then, the first stage is to find out which wire is affected, and to do this it is necessary to be able to read a wiring diagram. Such a diagram may, at first sight, appear disconcertingly like a plan of a railway marshalling yard—and, oddly enough, it is not at all a bad idea to think of it as such. The leads become railway lines, and the current the train which has to pass over them. Remember, though, that one important main line is not shown. This is the earth return, formed by the actual framework of the scooter itself. All the components are connected to this earth, which, therefore, forms one complete half of the circuit.

Where really complicated circuits are involved, it sometimes helps to trace them out individually, placing tracing paper over the wiring diagram and following the various lines until you have a picture of the complete circuit, with all its intermediate "stations" marked.

Having found the circuit, the next job is to check it. First, obviously, you have to discover whether any current is flowing or not, and here a test rig helps immensely. One can be made quite simply with a bulb, a bulb-holder, and a length of electrical lead. First, place the bulb-holder against one battery terminal, and then touch the other terminal with the end of the lead. The bulb should light. If not, it shows that the battery is flat, and it will have to be recharged before you can proceed.

Never forget that a flat battery is more likely to be a symptom of the trouble than the cause. There is almost certainly a short-circuit somewhere, which has caused the battery to drain itself. It is possible for this to be a short-circuit inside the battery itself, so get the garage to check its condition at the same time.

Once you are certain that the battery is all right you must check each individual lead in the circuit in question, a job made considerably easier by the fact that modern wiring harnesses use wires of distinctive colours for each of the individual circuits. Remember, though, that on the Vespa the battery *must* be disconnected whenever you intend to work on the lighting switch, for the reasons already explained.

So, in the case of the specimen circuit to the tail lamp, you would (having checked first the bulb and then the battery) have disconnected it temporarily while the lighting switch was opened up. The end of the lead would then be freed from its terminal, brought clear, and the battery reconnected. The test rig would then have been applied to the open end of the lead; the holder placed against the lead; and the holder wire connected to earth. If the lamp then lit, it would show that current was reaching the terminal. Disconnect the battery again, replace the lead you had removed, and remove the end of the tail-lamp lead from the switch. In its place connect the test-rig lead, and earth the holder. Connect the battery and operate the switch. If it lights the bulb the switch has a clean bill of health, and the fault must lie either in the tail-lamp lead or in the lamp itself.

Continue checking, stage by stage, throughout the entire circuit. You may find, for example, that when the test rig is connected to the lamp end of the terminal it will not light the bulb. This shows that the fault lies in the lead itself. It has probably fractured, so it must be traced and inspected minutely. If it is a simple fracture you will find two loose ends. Sometimes a short-circuit can be detected by switching on and shaking the machine. As the broken end earths itself a characteristic crackling of electricity can be heard.

More difficult to locate is an internal fracture, where the insulation is undamaged. Garage men use a test rig fitted with a needle-sharp probe which can be pushed through the insulation at various points until a stage is reached at which the test bulb fails to light. This can literally pin-point the position of the breakage. An alternative is to pull two ways on the lead, at intervals of about three inches, until a section is found which stretches under such treatment. This is the section in which the break has occurred.

Where the suspect lead is a very long one, or is inaccessible, a double check and a temporary repair can be made by connecting the two terminals with an external length of wire. Sometimes, a new lead can be drawn through the conduit by wiring it to the old lead and pulling it through with it.

When repairing fractured leads it is important to ensure that no undue electrical stresses are set up and that the insulation is made good. All joints should be twisted together as neatly as possible—it is even better if they can be soldered—and the new joint must be wound round with insulating tape to make leakage impossible. Any terminals which have been undone must be refitted tightly, and if a soldered joint has failed it *must* be resoldered. It is not sufficient to tape it up.

Given patience and a modicum of equipment, there is no reason why the average owner should not be able to trace most faults which can occur either in the engine or in the electrical system. Even when the nature of the failure is such that it is not possible to repair it oneself, it is often possible to provide a temporary cure, or at least to save money by giving the repairer an accurate diagnosis of the trouble.

TROUBLE TRACER

Those, then, are the methods to apply if trouble strikes on the road. And here is the factory's own basic trouble-tracing sequence, recommended for work both away from home and also in the garage.

Starting difficulties. Check the sparking plug. If it is not sparking, or if the spark is weak or irregular, then the following possibilities should be investigated—

1. Wrong grade of plug; 2. Plug gap incorrect; 3. Plug dirty or wet; 4. Plug "cooked;" 5. Plug cap tracking; 6. H.T. lead faulty; 7. Battery discharged or badly connected; 8. Rectifier faulty; 9. Contact-breaker points dirty, wet, or incorrectly gapped; 10. Ignition timing wrongly set; 11. Condensor faulty; 12. Coil faulty.

If the plug is sparking, check—

1. Is the choke opening properly? 2. Is the engine flooded? 3. Is the

carburettor float valve operating properly? 4. Are you starting without choke on a cold day? 5. Is there sufficient flow of fuel? 6. If not, are the filler cap breather and the fuel lines clear? 7. Is the petrol tap fully opened and is the tank full? 8. Are the carburettor internal passages clean?

If all these pass muster, go on to the checks in the next section.

Loss of power and performance. Check the compression by kicking the engine over. If the compression is bad—
1. The cylinder head joint is leaking; 2. The sparking plug is not properly screwed in; 3. The piston or rings are damaged, or the rings are sticking in their grooves.

If the compression is good, the power loss can be caused by—
1. Slack big-end bearings; 2. Damaged rotary valve seating; 3. Seizure or wear on main bearings; 4. In the case of bearing trouble, the root cause may be use of the wrong grade of oil or insufficient oil.

Noise and vibration. Vespa engines normally run quietly, and very smoothly. Excessive noise and/or vibration are indicative of trouble. The causes may be—
1. Running-in not properly carried out; 2. Overheating, caused by a build-up of dirt in the cooling fins or a damaged fan or cowl; 3. Sticking rings, leading to loss of compression and consequent overheating and bad starting; 5. Excessive carbon deposits, especially in the exhaust port and silencer. This could be due to the use of too much oil, or of a thicker grade than recommended.

Transmission trouble. Any shortcomings in the clutch or gearbox are likely to be the result of actual damage to the parts themselves. Clutch snatch or slip and faulty operation of the gearbox may be due to improper lubrication. It is important to see that the gearbox oil does not fall below the correct level, since it feeds the gearbox, clutch and the clutch side main bearing. In all, the box should contain 250 c.c. of oil, save on models up to VSB 1 M-009501, where the filler is lower and 180 c.c. suffices.

Suspension bottoming. There are two possible causes of bottoming on Vespa front suspension systems. They are—
1. On Models prior to GS VSB 1 T-008019, fit the latest type of damper in place of the old one. This has superior damping qualities on bump; 2. Check the rubber buffers. These should be of cylindrical pattern. If they are not, replace them with the latest type.

Excessive fuel consumption. Carry out all the checks detailed on the ignition and carburation, and see that the engine compression is good and that there is no excessive carbon. Check, also that the air intake under the seat is not blocked or choked by rags, etc.

CHECK POINTS

These are the most important points to check when tracing troubles—

Engine. Tightness of nuts and bolts; grade of plug; grade and percentage of oil; contact-breaker gap (0·5 mm = 0·019-in.); timing 26° b.t.d.c. ± 1° on both the VSB 1 and 180 SS; 27° ± 1° on the high-compression version of the VS 5; 31° ± 1° on earlier VS 5s and all previous models; setting of control cables.

Battery and lights. Condition of rectifier; condition of fuse; security of terminal connections; battery connected correctly; insulation of leads intact and terminals unoxidized; bulb contacts clean and tight; horn regulating screw properly set.

Brakes. Controls properly set and working freely; brake drums unscored and not oval; brake shoe linings not excessively worn; oil seals in order.

Steering. Check the steering head bearing setting; listen for faulty bearing balls or "gritty" races; test the security of all wheel nuts; check the wheel bearings for play.

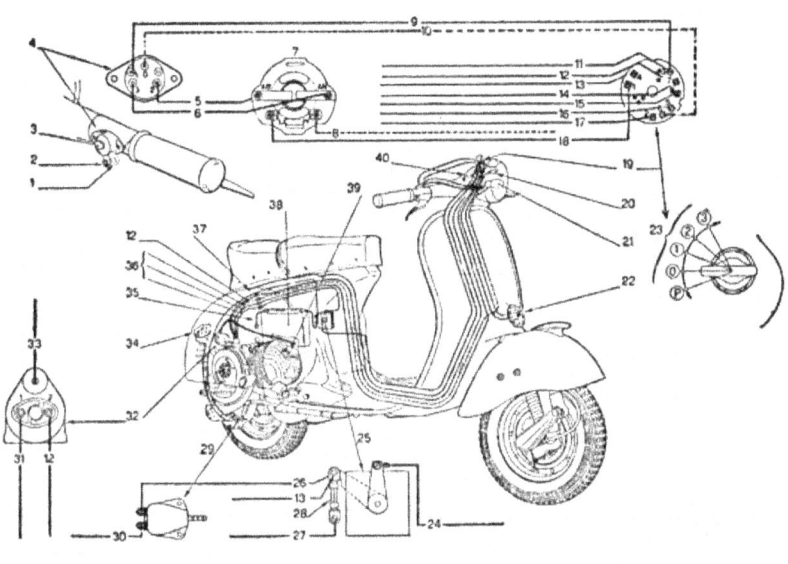
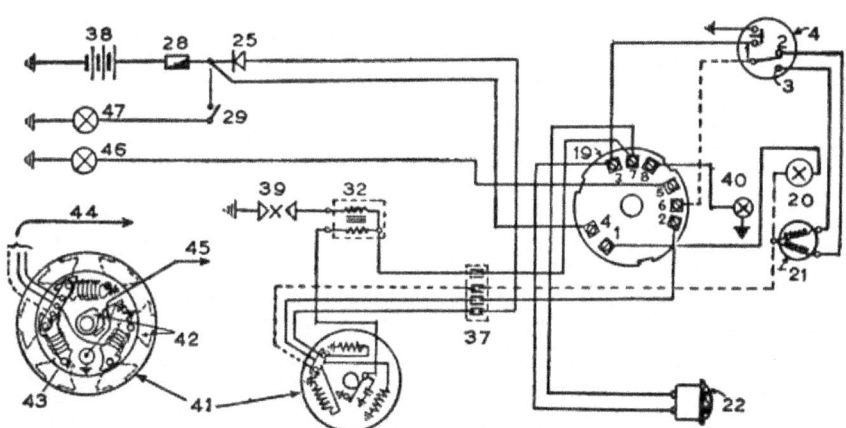

Fig. 34. Wiring Diagram, G.S. Vespa Series VS 2

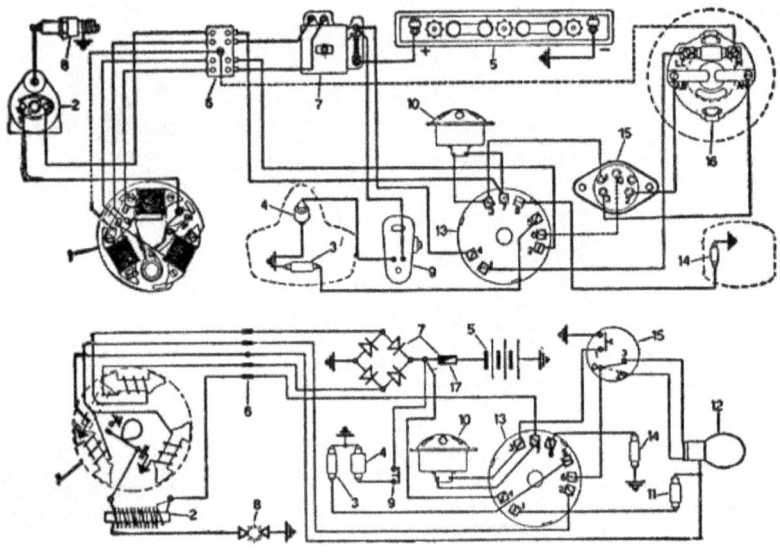

Fig. 35. Wiring Diagram, G.S. Vespa VS 4

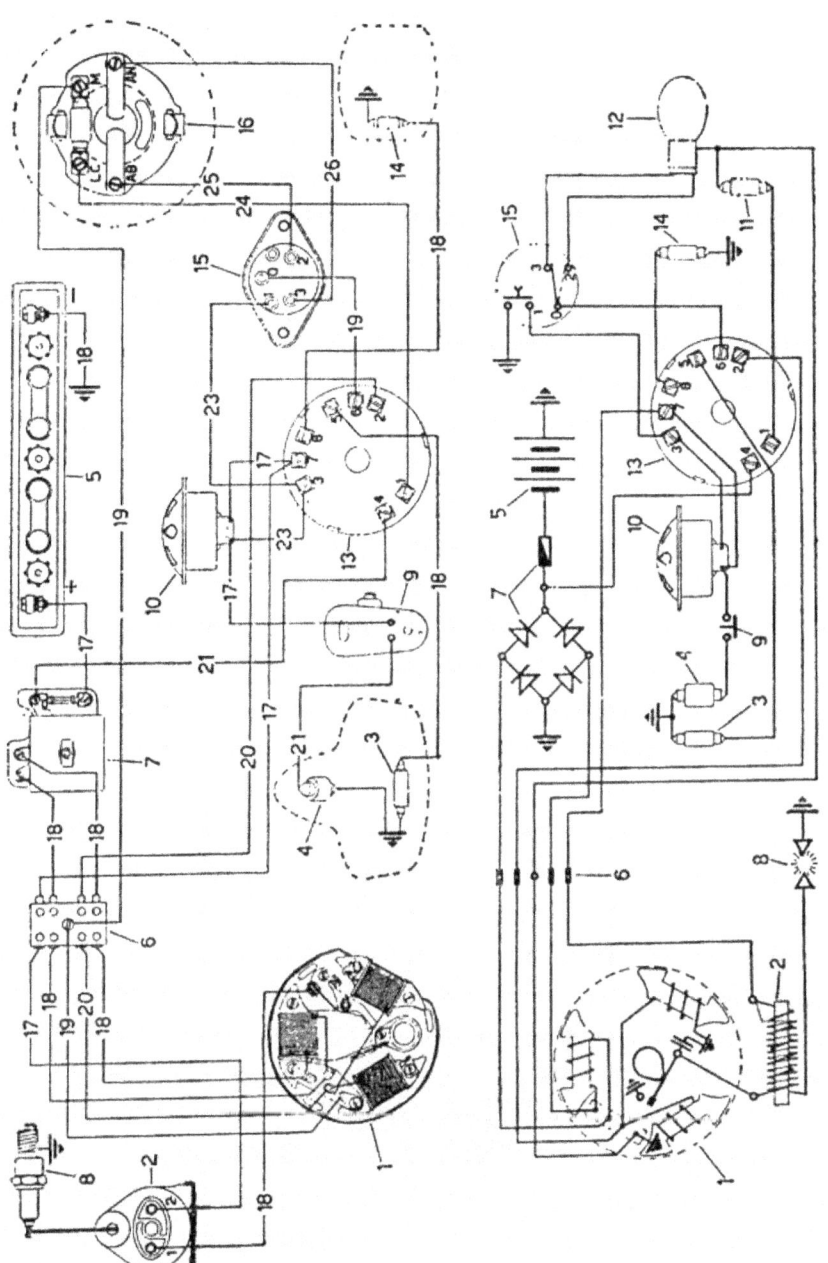

Fig. 36. Wiring Diagram, G.S. Vespa VS5 Series

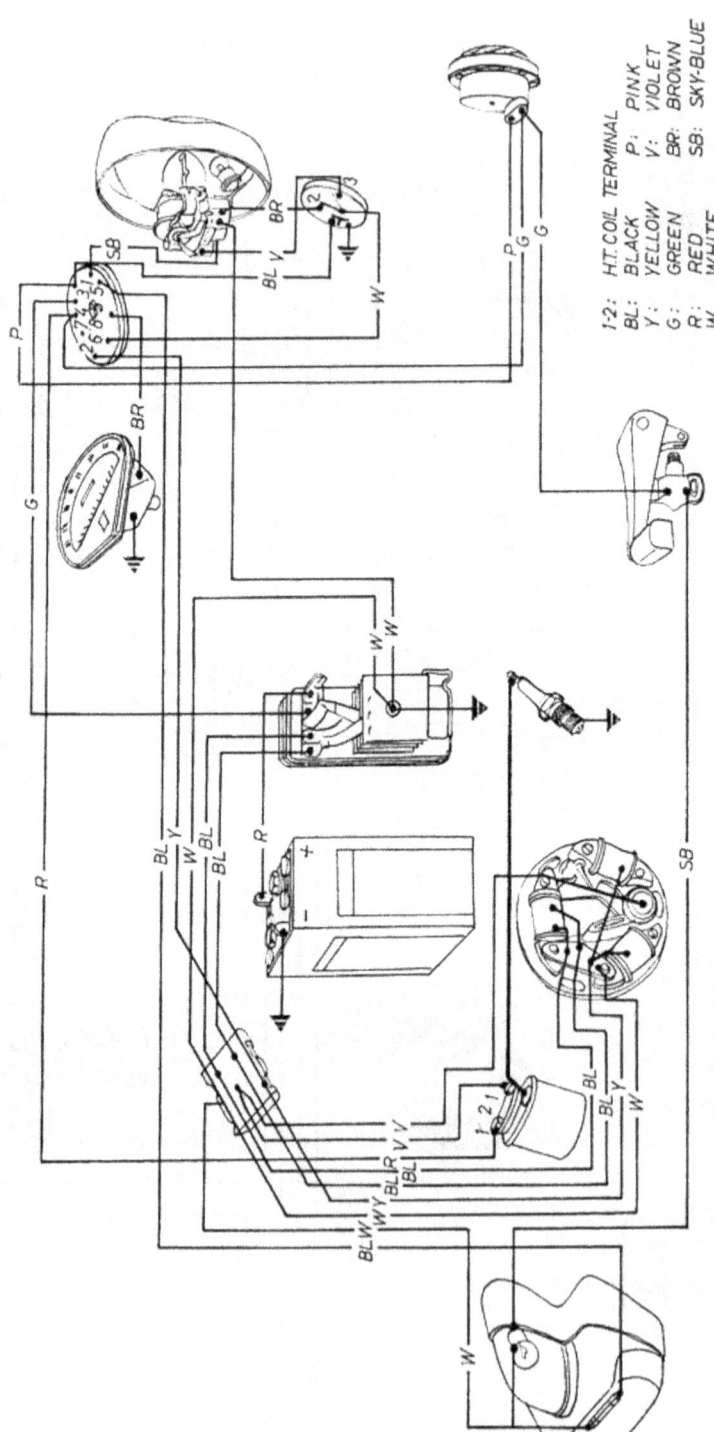

Fig. 37a. Wiring Diagram, VSB 1 with Battery

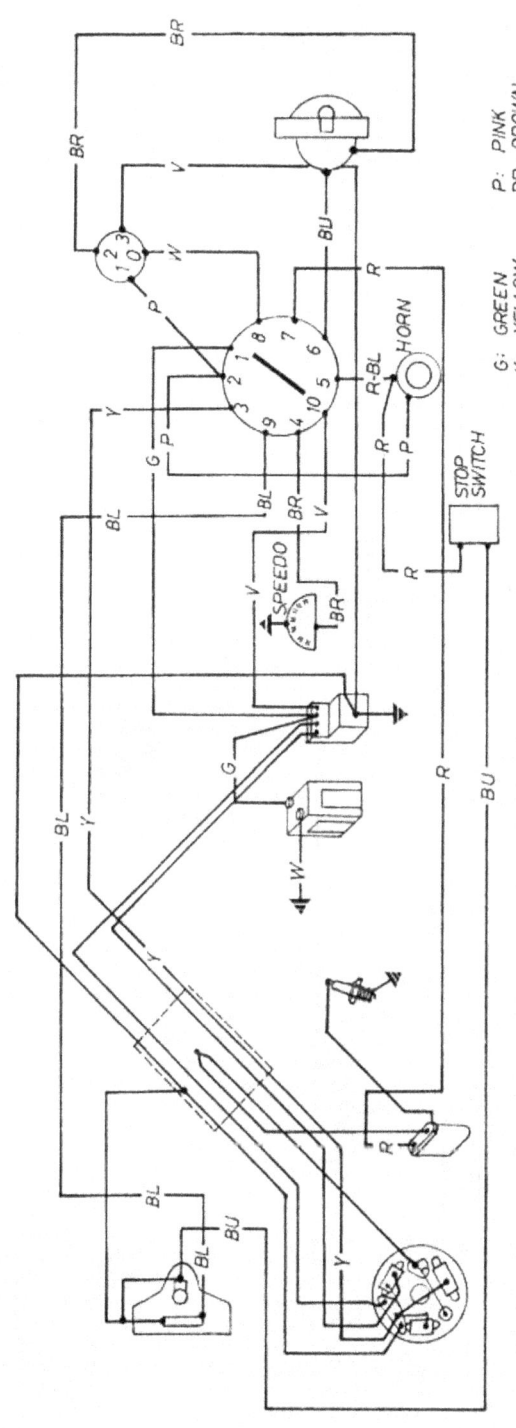

Fig. 37B. Wiring Diagram, G.S. Models VSB 1 Series 2

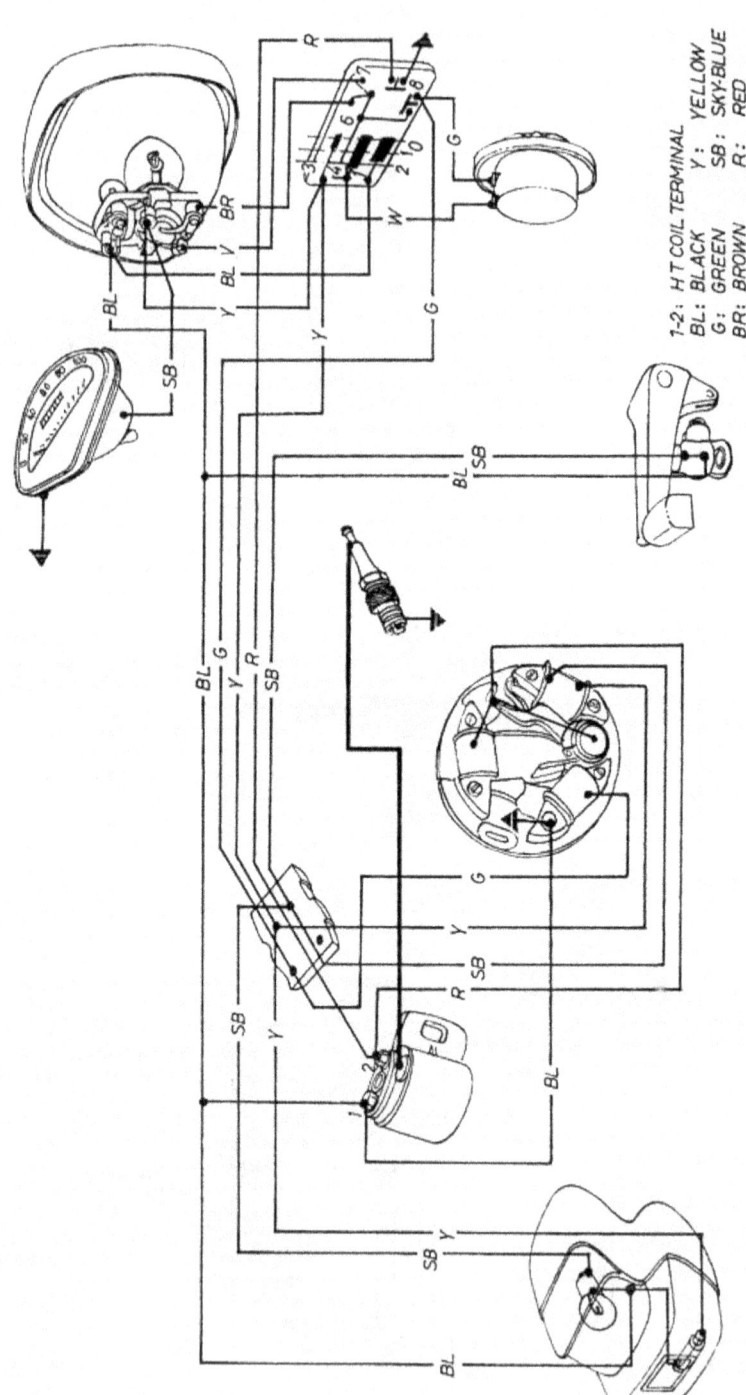

Fig. 38A. Wiring Diagram, VSB 1 without Battery

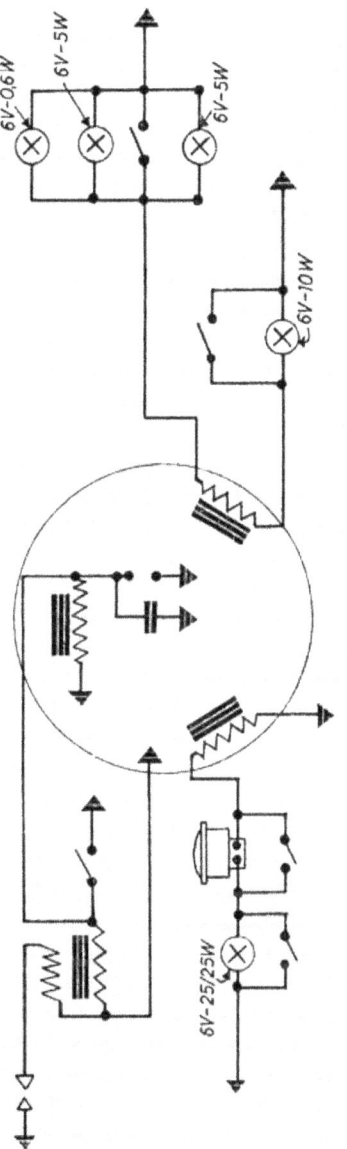

Fig. 38b. Wiring Diagram, 180 SS without Battery

APPENDIX

MAINTENANCE AND LUBRICATION (ALL MODELS)—1

Group	OPERATIONS TO CARRY OUT				Lubricant	Notes
	After first 600 miles	After 2,400 miles	Every 4,800 miles	During overhauls		
Gearbox	Oil change (**) Check and top up after first 1,200 miles	Oil change (**) Check and top up after subsequent 1,200 miles	Oil change (**)	Oil change (**)	Esso Motor Oil 30 Shell X-100 Motor Oil 2 T Shell X-100 Motor Oil 30 Mobiloil A	(**) Operations to be carried out with warm engine. Clean magnetic drain plug.
Gear Selector	—	Grease	Grease	Grease	Esso Multi Purpose Grease "H" or Grease 2 Shell Retinax A Shell Alvania Grease 3 Mobilgrease MP Mobilgrease Special	
Brake lever and pedal fulcrum points Front suspension Felt pad on fly-wheel cam	—	Grease	—	Grease		
Air Filter	Clean in petrol and dry in air jet	Clean in petrol and dry in air jet	—	Clean in petrol and dry in air jet	—	The filter should be cleaned more regularly when running on dusty roads.
Speedometer drive system Control cables	—	—	Grease (°°)	Grease (°°)	Esso Multi Purpose Grease "H" or Grease 2 Shell Retinax A Shell Alvania Grease 3 Mobilgrease MP Mobilgrease Special	(°°) Use 75% of ESSO SAE 30 plus 25% Esso Multi-Purpose Grease 2 for lubricating control cables.
More important bolts and nuts	Check tightness	—	—	Check tightness	—	
Sparking plug	—	Clean, and adjust electrode gap to 0·6 mm (0·023 in.)	—	Fit new sparking plug	—	

MAINTENANCE AND LUBRICATION (ALL MODELS)—2

Group	OPERATIONS TO CARRY OUT					Lubricant	Notes
	After first 600 miles	Every 2,400 miles	Every 4,800 miles	During overhauls			
Silencer	—	Clean exhaust pipe (++) (*Piaggio recommendation*)	Clean exhaust pipe (++) (*Douglas recommendation*)	Clean exhaust pipe (++)	—	(++) Clean using a hooked wire or by burning out - carbon. (*See also* page 42.)
Engine	Check carburettor nuts and bolts for tightness	Decoke piston, cylinder head, cylinder ports (*Piaggio recommendation*)	Decoke piston, cylinder head, cylinder ports (*Douglas recommendation*)	Decoke engine parts. To be reassembled	—	The outlet section of the pipe is at least 10 mm (0·4 in.) wide.
Flywheel	—	—	Clean contact-breaker points and adjust gap to 0·019 in.; check timing	Replace contact-breaker arm (if necessary) or clean and set points; check timing	—	
Main bearing housing, flywheel side	—	—	—	Introduce 6 c.c. of grease after cleaning out the housing with petrol	Esso Multi Purpose Grease 2 Shell Alvania Grease 3 Mobilgrease Special	
Bearings and area of speedometer bearing on front wheel axle	—	—	—	Grease	Esso Multi Purpose Grease "H" or Grease 2 Shell Retinax A Shell Alvania Grease 3 Mobilgrease MP Mobilgrease Special	
Battery	Periodically add distilled water (once a month or depending on distance of runs and seasonal temperatures) so that the plates are always immersed.					

When the vehicle is to be left inactive over a long period carry out the following instructions: 1. Clean the vehicle – 2. With engine stationary and throttle open, introduce 40 c.c. Esso Motor Oil 30 (Shell X-100 Motor Oil 2T, Shell X-100 Motor Oil 30 or Mobiloil A); actuate kick-starter 3 or 4 times – 3. Drain off all fuel – 4. Grease all unpainted metallic parts – 5. Disconnect battery cables, clean poles and dry – 6. Raise the vehicle wheels from the ground.

LUBRICATION CHART 150 c.c. MODELS

Parts to be lubricated		Lubrication			
		Shell	*B.P.*	*Esso*	*Mobil*
Every 2,400 miles	Every 4,800 miles				
Gearbox topping-up	Gearbox change oil	Shell 2T Two-Stroke Oil or Shell X-100 30	Energol Two-Stroke Oil or Energol S.A.E. 30	Esso Extra Motor Oil 20W/30	Mobiloil A
Control cables Front suspension Felt pad on flywheel cam Joints on brake control Speedo flexible drive	Gearchange quadrant	Retinax A	Energrease L.2	Esso Multi-Purpose Grease H	Mobilgrease M.P.
Engine at each refuelling		Shell 2T Two-Stroke Oil in ratio of 6% or ½ pint to 1 gal petrol	Energol Two-Stroke Oil in ratio of 6% or ½ pint to 1 gal petrol	Essolube 30 in ratio of 6% or ½ pint to 1 gal petrol. Esso Two-Stroke Motor Oil in ratio of ¾ pint to 1 gal petrol	Mobiloil A in ratio of 6% or ½ pint to 1 gal petrol. Mobil-Mix in ratio of ¾ pint to 1 gal petrol
					Castrol XL in ratio of 6% or ½ pint to 1 gal petrol. Castrol Two-Stroke Oil in ratio of ¾ pint to 1 gal petrol

* Marketed also by National Benzole Co. Ltd., by arrangement with Shell-Mex & B.P. Ltd.

LUBRICATION CHART 160 c.c. MODELS

Part to be lubricated		Lubrication				
Every 2,400 miles	Every 4,300 miles	**Shell*	**B.P.*	*Esso*	*Castrol*	*Mobil*
Gearbox topping-up	Gearbox change oil	Shell 2T Two-Stroke Oil or Shell X-100 30	Energol Two-Stroke Oil or Energol S.A.E. 30	Esso Extra Motor Oil 20W/30	Castrol XL	Mobiloil A
Front suspension Felt pad on flywheel cam Joints on brake control Speedo flexible drive	Control cables Gearchange quadrant	Retinax A	Energrease L.2	Esso Multi-Purpose Grease H	Castrolease L.M.	Mobilgrease M.P.
Engine at each re-fuelling		Shell 2T Two-Stroke Oil in ratio of 5% or ½ pint to 1¼ galls. petrol	Energol Two-Stroke Oil in ratio of 5% or ½ pint to 1¼ galls. petrol	Essolube 30 in ratio of 5% or ½ pint to 1¼ galls. petrol. Esso Two-Stroke Motor Oil in ratio of ¾ pint to 1¼ galls. petrol	Castrol XL in ratio of 5% or ½ pint to 1¼ galls. petrol. Castrol Two-Stroke Oil in ratio of ¾ pint to 1¼ galls. petrol	Mobiloil A in ratio of 5% or ½ pint to 1¼ galls. petrol or Mobil-Mix in ratio of ¾ pint to 1¼ galls. petrol

* Marketed also by National Benzole Co. Ltd., by arrangement with B.P. & Shell-Mex Ltd.

APPROVED PETROL/OIL MIXTURE

Make	*Description*
Shell	2T Two-Stroke Mixture
B.P.	B.P.-Zoom
National Benzole Co. Ltd.	Hi-Fli

Hydraulic Dampers	When not working efficiently, consult your Dealer. If servicing is required, they should always be returned to the Works.

LUBRICATION CHART 180 c.c. MODELS

Part to be lubricated		Lubrication				
		*Shell	*B.P.	Esso	Castrol	Mobil
Every 2,400 miles	Gearbox topping-up	Shell 2T Two-Stroke Oil or Shell X-100 30	Energol Two-Stroke Oil or Energol S.A.E. 30	Esso Extra Motor Oil 20W/30	Castrol XL	Mobiloil A
Every 4,800 miles	Control Cables Gearchange quadrant	Retinax A	Energrease L.2	Esso Multi-Purpose Grease H	Castrolease L.M.	Mobilgrease M.P.
Front suspension Felt pad on flywheel cam Joints on brake control Speedo flexible drive						
Engine at each re-fuelling		Shell 2T Two-Stroke Oil in ratio of 5% or ½-pint to 1¼-galls. petrol	Energol Two-Stroke Oil in ratio of 5% or ½-pint to 1¼-galls. petrol	Essolube 30 in ratio of 5% or ½-pint to 1¼-galls. petrol. Esso Two-Stoke Motor Oil in ratio of ¾-pint to 1¼-galls. petrol	Castrol XL in ratio of 5% or ½-pint to 1¼-galls. petrol Castrol Two-Stroke Oil in ratio of ¾-pint to 1¼-galls. petrol	Mobiloil A in ratio of 5% or ½-pint to 1¼-galls. petrol or Mobil-Mix in ratio of ¾-pint to 1¼-galls. petrol

* Marketed also by National Benzole Co. Ltd., by arrangement with B.P. & Shell-Mex Ltd.

The greases specified on this chart should also be used for the speedometer pinion and front wheel bearings and for the main bearing of the F/side of c/shaft during overhaul.

APPROVED PETROL/OIL MIXTURE

Make	Description
Shell	2T Two-Stroke Mixture
B.P.	B.P.-Zoom
National Benzole Co. Ltd.	Hi-Fli

PLUG RECOMMENDATIONS

	Champion	Bosch	Lodge	KLG	Marelli
150 c.c.	N 84	—	2HLN	FE 80	—
160 c.c.					
180 c.c.	NA 8	W 240 T2	2H LN	FE 80	CW 250 L-T CW 240 G CW 240 B

Plug gaps 0·020–0·026-in.

TYRE PRESSURES

		Solo	Pillion
150 c.c.	Front	16 lb per sq in.	16 lb per sq in.
	Rear	20 ,,	32 ,,
160 c.c.	Front	16 ,,	20 ,,
	Rear	16 ,,	32 ,,
180 c.c.	Front	17 ,,	17 ,,
	Rear	25 ,,	35 ,,

INDEX

AIR filter, cleaning, 72
   removal, 35, 36, 45

BATTERY, care of, 50
   terminals, 51
   topping up, 73
Brake adjustment—
   front, 53
   rear, 54
   cables, renewal, 54
Brakes, operation, 24
   testing, 3
Bulbs, checking, 51

CARBURETTOR, air filter, 16
   cleaning, 45
   construction, 13
   cross-section, 15
   "exploded," 14
   stripping, 45, 46
Clutch, adjustment, 55
   "exploded," 21
   operation, 20, 22
   overhaul, 1
   removal, 43, 44
   stripping, 44
Contact breaker, adjustment, 47, 48
   checking, 59, 60
   cleaning, 48
   lubrication, 49
   periodic care, 73
   renewing, 49
Crankcase, splitting, 44
Cylinder barrel, removal, 39
Cylinder cowl, removal, 36
Cylinder head, decarbonizing, 38
   removal, 36, 37

DAMPER, operation, 22
Decarbonizing, 1, 34–43
   exhaust port, 38
   head, 38
   intervals, 35, 73

Decarbonizing (*contd.*)—
   piston, 38, 41
   rebuilding after, 43
   ring grooves, 40, 41
   rings, 41
   silencer, 42
   spares needed, 35
   tools, 35
Demagnetization, 49

ENGINE, construction, 5, 7
   cutaway view, 6
   "exploded," 5
   four-stroke cycle, 8
   induction system, 11
   lubrication, 12, 13
   stripping, 43, 44
   two-stroke cycle, 9
Exhaust port, access, 38
   decarbonizing, 38, 39
Exhaust smoke, 60
Exhaust system, removal, 38

FAN cowl, detaching, 35
Front brake, *see* BRAKE

GEAR cable, failure, 55
Gearbox, drain plug, 32
   filler plug, 32
   oil level, 55, 56
   operation, 20
General layout, 2
Gudgeon pin, removal, 39, 40

IDLING, setting, 46
Ignition system, 16, 17, 18, 19
   timing, 71

JETS, cleaning, 45
   renewal, 45

LENSES, purpose, 51
Lubrication, controls, 72

INDEX

Lubrication (*contd.*)—
  data, 150 cc., 74
  data, 160 cc., 75
  data, 180 cc., 76
  main bearings, 73
  points, 29, 31

MAINTENANCE, daily checks, 30
  weekly checks, 30

OILS, changes, 72
  recommended, 72

PINKING, 60
Piston, decarbonizing, 38, 39
  removal, 39, 40
Piston rings, checking, 41
  gap, 41, 42
  removal, 40
Plugs, care of, 72
  gaps, 77
  recommended, 77
  washer, renewal, 43

REFLECTOR, tarnished, 51
Ring grooves, cleaning, 40, 41

SCOOTER, laying up, 73
Short circuits, 60
Silencer, cleaning, 73
  decarbonizing, 42
Spark, checking, 59
Sparking plug, *see* PLUGS

Specific gravity, checking, 50
Speedometer drive, lubrication, 72
Steering, operation, 22
Suspension, "exploded," 22
  operation, 22
Switches, lubrication, 51

TAB washers, 32
Test lamp, 61
Timing, setting, 49, 50
Tools, 25–27
Trouble tracing, factory method, 62–71
  general procedure, 58–60
Tyres, care of, 56, 57
  pressures, 77

VENT, cleaning, 44

WHEELS, bearings, 73
  rims, 56
Wiring diagram, interpreting, 61
  VS 2, 65
  VS 4, 66
  VS 5, 67
  VSB 1 with battery, 68
  VSB 1 Series 2, 69
  VSB 1 without battery, 70
  180 SS without battery, 71
Wiring loom, repairs, 51
Workshop manual, 3

> **ARE YOU:**
> **INTERESTED IN EUROPEAN, IMPORT & EXOTIC AUTOMOBILES?**
>
> **DO YOU:**
> **DO YOUR OWN MAINTENANCE?**
>
> If you answered yes to either of these questions, then you should check out our automobile books and manuals. We have included a sample listing of some of our featured marques. However, for complete details and the most up-to-date information, please visit our website.
>
> ——— www.VelocePress.com ———
>
> The fastest growing specialist USA publisher of niche market automotive books and manuals.
>
> All VelocePress titles are available through your local independent bookseller, Amazon.com or direct from VelocePress. Wholesale customers may also purchase direct or from the Ingram Book Group.

AUTOBOOKS WORKSHOP MANUALS

ALFA ROMEO GIULIA 1300, 1600, 1750, 2000 1962-1978 WSM
AUSTIN HEALEY SPRITE, MG MIDGET 1958-1980 WSM
BMW 1600 1966-1973 WSM
BMW 2000 & 2002 1966-1976 WSM
BMW 2500, 2800, 3.0 & 3.3 1968-1977 WSM
BMW 316, 320, 320i 1975-1977 WSM
BMW 518, 520, 520i 1973-1981 WSM
FIAT 1100, 1100D, 1100R & 1200 1957-1969 WSM
FIAT 124 1966-1974 WSM
FIAT 124 SPORT 1966-1975 WSM
FIAT 125 & 125 SPECIAL 1967-1973 WSM
FIAT 126, 126L, 126 DV, 126/650 & 126/650 DV 1972-1982 WSM
FIAT 127 SALOON, SPECIAL & SPORT, 900, 1050 1971-1981 WSM
FIAT 128 1969-1982 WSM
FIAT 1300, 1500 1961-1967 WSM
FIAT 131 MIRAFIORI 1975-1982 WSM
FIAT 132 1972-1982 WSM
FIAT 500 1957-1973 WSM
FIAT 600, 600D & MULTIPLA 1955-1969 WSM
FIAT 850 1964-1972 WSM
JAGUAR E-TYPE 1961-1972 WSM
JAGUAR MK 1, 2 1955-1969 WSM
JAGUAR S TYPE, 420 1963-1968 WSM
JAGUAR XK 120, 140, 150 MK 7, 8, 9 1948-1961 WSM
LAND ROVER 1, 2 1948-1961 WSM
MERCEDES-BENZ 190 1959-1968 WSM
MERCEDES-BENZ 220/8 1968-1972 WSM
MERCEDES-BENZ 220B 1959-1965 WSM
MERCEDES-BENZ 230 1963-1968 WSM
MERCEDES-BENZ 250 1968-1972 WSM
MERCEDES-BENZ 280 1968-1972 WSM
MG MIDGET TA-TF 1936-1955 WSM
MINI 1959-1980 WSM
MORRIS MINOR 1952-1971 WSM
PEUGEOT 404 1960-1975 WSM
PORSCHE 911 1964-1973 WSM
PORSCHE 911 1970-1977 WSM
RENAULT 16 1965-1979 WSM
RENAULT 8, 10, 1100 1962-1971 WSM
ROVER 3500, 3500S 1968-1976 WSM
SUNBEAM RAPIER, ALPINE 1955-1965 WSM
TRIUMPH SPITFIRE, GT6, VITESSE 1962-1968 WSM
TRIUMPH TR2, TR3, TR3A 1952-1962 WSM
TRIUMPH TR4, TR4A 1961-1967 WSM
VOLKSWAGEN BEETLE 1968-1977 WSM

BROOKLANDS BOOKS & ROAD TEST PORTFOLIOS (RTP)

AC CARS 1904-2009
ALFA ROMEO 1920-1933 ROAD TEST PORTFOLIO
ALFA ROMEO 1934-1940 ROAD TEST PORTFOLIO
BRABHAM RALT HONDA THE RON TAURANAC STORY
BUGATTI TYPE 10 TO TYPE 40 ROAD TEST PORTFOLIO
BUGATTI TYPE 10 TO TYPE 251 ROAD TEST PORTFOLIO
BUGATTI TYPE 41 TO TYPE 55 ROAD TEST PORTFOLIO
BUGATTI TYPE 57 TO TYPE 251 ROAD TEST PORTFOLIO
DELAHAYE ROAD TEST PORTFOLIO
FERRARI ROAD CARS 1946-1956 ROAD TEST PORTFOLIO
FIAT 500 1936-1972 ROAD TEST PORTFOLIO
FIAT DINO ROAD TEST PORTFOLIO
HISPANO SUIZA ROAD TEST PORTFOLIO
HONDA ST1100/ST1300 PAN EUROPEAN 1990-2002 RTP
JAGUAR MK1 & MK2 ROAD TEST PORTFOLIO
LOTUS CORTINA ROAD TEST PORTFOLIO
MV AGUSTA F4 750 & 1000 1997-2007 ROAD TEST PORTFOLIO
TATRA CARS ROAD TEST PORTFOLIO

VELOCEPRESS AUTOMOBILE BOOKS & MANUALS

ABARTH BUYERS GUIDE
AUSTIN-HEALEY 6-CYLINDER WSM
BMW 600 LIMOUSINE FACTORY WSM
BMW 600 LIMOUSINE OWNERS HAND BOOK & SERVICE MANUAL
BMW ISETTA FACTORY WSM
BOOK OF THE CARRERA PANAMERICANA - MEXICAN ROAD RACE
COMPLETE CATALOG OF JAPANESE MOTOR VEHICLES
DIALED IN - THE JAN OPPERMAN STORY
FERRARI 250/GT SERVICE AND MAINTENANCE
FERRARI 308 SERIES BUYER'S AND OWNER'S GUIDE
FERRARI BERLINETTA LUSSO
FERRARI BROCHURES AND SALES LITERATURE 1946-1967
FERRARI BROCHURES AND SALES LITERATURE 1968-1989
FERRARI GUIDE TO PERFORMANCE
FERRARI OPP, MAINTENANCE & SERVICE H/BOOKS 1948-1963
FERRARI OWNER'S HANDBOOK
FERRARI SERIAL NUMBERS PART I - ODD NUMBERS TO 21399
FERRARI SERIAL NUMBERS PART II - EVEN NUMBERS TO 1050
FERRARI SPYDER CALIFORNIA
FERRARI TUNING TIPS & MAINTENANCE TECHNIQUES
HENRY'S FABULOUS MODEL "A" FORD
HOW TO BUILD A FIBERGLASS CAR
HOW TO BUILD A RACING CAR
HOW TO RESTORE THE MODEL 'A' FORD
IF HEMINGWAY HAD WRITTEN A RACING NOVEL
JAGUAR E-TYPE 3.8 & 4.2 WSM
LE MANS 24 (THE BOOK THAT THE FILM WAS BASED ON)
MASERATI BROCHURES AND SALES LITERATURE
MASERATI OWNER'S HANDBOOK
METROPOLITAN FACTORY WSM
MGA & MGB OWNERS HANDBOOK & WSM
OBERT'S FIAT GUIDE
PERFORMANCE TUNING THE SUNBEAM TIGER
PORSCHE 356 1948-1965 WSM
PORSCHE 912 WSM
SOUPING THE VOLKSWAGEN
TRIUMPH TR2, TR3, TR4 1953-1965 WSM
VEDA ORR'S NEW REVISED HOT ROD PICTORIAL
VOLKSWAGEN TRANSPORTER, TRUCKS, STATION WAGONS WSM
VOLVO 1944-1968 ALL MODELS WSM

VELOCEPRESS MOTORCYCLE BOOKS & MANUALS

AJS SINGLES 1955-65 350cc & 500cc (BOOK OF)
ARIEL 1939-1960 4 STROKE SINGLES (BOOK OF)
ARIEL LEADER & ARROW 1958-1964 (BOOK OF)
ARIEL MOTORCYCLES 1933-1951 WSM
ARIEL PREWAR MODELS 1932-1939 (BOOK OF)
BMW M/CYCLES R26 R27 (1956-1967) FACTORY WSM
BMW M/CYCLES R50 R50S R60 R69S (1955-1969) FACTORY WSM
BSA BANTAM (BOOK OF)
BSA ALL FOUR-STROKE SINGLES & V-TWINS 1936-1952 (BOOK OF)
BSA OHV & SV SINGLES - 250cc 1954-1970 (BOOK OF)
BSA OHV & SV SINGLES 1945-54 250-600cc (BOOK OF)
BSA OHV SINGLES 350 & 500cc 1955-1967 (BOOK OF)
BSA PRE-WAR MODELS TO 1939 (BOOK OF)
BSA TWINS 1948-1962 (BOOK OF)
BSA TWINS 1962-1969 (SECOND BOOK OF)
CATALOG OF BRITISH MOTORCYCLES (1951 MODELS)
DOUGLAS PRE-WAR ALL MODELS 1929-1939 (BOOK OF)
DOUGLAS POST-WAR ALL MODELS 1948-1957 FACTORY WSM
DUCATI 160cc, 250cc & 350cc OHC MODELS FACTORY WSM
HONDA 50 ALL MODELS UP TO 1970 INC MONKEY & TRAIL (BOOK OF)
HONDA 90 ALL MODELS UP TO 1966 (BOOK OF)
HONDA MOTORCYCLES 125-150 TWINS C/CS/CB/CA WSM
HONDA MOTORCYCLES 250-305 TWINS C/CS/CB WSM
HONDA MOTORCYCLES C100 SUPER CUB WSM
HONDA MOTORCYCLES C110 SPORT CUB 1962-1969 WSM
HONDA TWINS & SINGLES 50cc TO 305cc 1960-1966 (BOOK OF)
HONDA TWINS ALL MODELS 125cc THRU 450cc UP TO 1968 (BOOK OF)
INDIAN PONYBIKE, BOY RACER & PAPOOSE ILL PARTS LIST & SALES LIT
LAMBRETTA ALL 125 & 150cc MODELS 1947-1957 (BOOK OF)
LAMBRETTA LI & TV MODELS 1957-1970 (SECOND BOOK OF)
MATCHLESS 350 & 500cc SINGLES 1945-1956 (BOOK OF)
MATCHLESS 350 & 500cc SINGLES 1955-1966 (BOOK OF)
NORTON 1938-1956 (BOOK OF)
NORTON DOMINATOR TWINS 1955-1965 (BOOK OF)
NORTON MODELS 19, 50 & ES2 1955-1963 (BOOK OF)
NORTON MOTORCYCLES 1957-1970 FACTORY WSM
NORTON PREWAR MODELS 1932-1939 (BOOK OF)
ROYAL ENFIELD 736cc INTERCEPTOR FACTORY WSM
ROYAL ENFIELD 250cc & 350cc SINGLES 1958-1966 (SECOND BOOK OF)
SUZUKI 50cc & 80cc UP TO 1966 (BOOK OF)
SUZUKI T10 1963-1967 FACTORY WSM
SUZUKI T20 & T200 1965-1969 FACTORY WSM
TRIUMPH PRE-WAR MOTORCYCLE 1935-1939 (BOOK OF)
TRIUMPH MOTORCYCLES 1937-1951 WSM
TRIUMPH MOTORCYCLES 1945-1955 FACTORY WSM
TRIUMPH TWINS 1956-1969 (BOOK OF)
VELOCETTE ALL SINGLES & TWINS 1925-1970 (BOOK OF)
VESPA 1951-1961 (BOOK OF)
VESPA GS & SS 1955-1968 (BOOK OF)
VINCENT MOTORCYCLES 1935-1955 WSM

www.VelocePress.com

www.ingramcontent.com/pod-product-compliance
Lightning Source LLC
Chambersburg PA
CBHW060350190426
43201CB00043B/1905